BRITISH MILITARY
AIRCRAFT
ACCIDENTS
THE LAST 25 YEARS

BRITISH MILITARY AIRCRAFT ACCIDENTS

THE LAST 25 YEARS

DAVID OLIVER

LONDON

IAN ALLAN LTD

First published 1990

ISBN 0 7110 1786 7

Published by Ian Allan Ltd, Shepperton, Surrey; and printed by Ian Allan Printing Ltd at their works at Coombelands in Runnymede, England

Frontispiece:
Harrier GR3 XZ989 of No 1 Squadron after making a forced landing at Port San Carlos, 8 June 1982. *815 Sqn*

Previous page:
Canberra E15 WH972 of No 100 Squadron which crashed in bad weather near RAF Kinloss on 27 June 1990. *Dave Morgan*

Cover:
Phantom FG1 XV589 of No 111 Squadron was abandoned on approach to RAF Alconbury following opening of the nose radome in flight, 3 June 1980. *S. Donald*

Acknowledgements

The author would like to express his thanks to the members of the armed services and other individuals for their assistance and co-operation during the preparation of this book, with particular thanks to:

Gp Capt I. K. McKee AFC, RAF,
  Inspectorate of Flight Safety
Lt-Cdr P. Barton RN,
  Royal Navy Aircraft Accident
  Investigation Unit
Cdr D. H. N. Yates RN,
  Royal Navy Flight Safety Centre
Lt-Col R. C. Baynes MBE, AAC,
  Army Air Corps Aviation
  Standards Branch
W. H. Tench CBE
Dave Allport
A. J. Goodrum
Bill Chorley
Peter Cooper

Categories of Military Accidents

Category 3:
> The aircraft damage is considered to be beyond unit resources but may be repairable on site by a Service working party or a contractor's working party

Category 4:
> The aircraft damage is considered to need special facilities or equipment for repair which is not available on site

Category 5:
> The aircraft is considered to be damaged beyond economical repair

Contents

Abbreviations

AAC	Army Air Corps	HUD	Head-Up Display
A&AEE	Aeroplane & Armament Experimental Establishment	I	Injured
		LFA	Low Flying Area
		LTF	Lightning Training Flight
AAIU	Aircraft Accident Investigation Unit	NAVEX	Navigation Exercise
		NI	Northern Ireland
ADR	Aircraft Data Recorder	NOM	Normal Operating Manoeuvre
AE	Aircrew Error		
AEF	Air Experience Flight	NPD	Non-Pilot Default
AFB	Air Force Base	NVG	Night Vision Goggles
AIB	Accident Investigation Branch	OCU	Operational Conversion Unit
ARWS	Advanced Rotary Wing Squadron	RAE	Royal Aeroplane Establishment
BATUS	British Army Training Unit Support	RAFC	RAF College
		RDG	Royal Dragoon Guards
BRNC	Britannia Royal Naval College	RHA	Royal Horse Artillery
		RNAS	RN Air Station
CASEVAC	Casualty Evacuation	RNEFTS	RN Elementary Flying Training School
CBAS	Commando Brigade Air Squadron	SAR	Search & Rescue
CFS	Central Flying School	SE	Service Error
DBR	Damaged Beyond Repair	Sqn	Squadron
Ej	Ejected	TD	Technical Defect
ETPS	Empire Test Pilots School	TTF	Tanker Task Force
F	Fatalities	TTTE	Tri-National Tornado Training Establishment
FARELF	Far East Liaison Flight		
Flt	Flight	TWCU	Tornado Weapons Conversion Unit
FRA	First-Run Attack		
FRADU	Fleet Requirements & Direction Unit	TWU	Tactical Weapons Unit
		UAS	University Air Squadron
FTS	Flying Training School	UNFIYCYP	UN Forces Cyprus
FOD	Foreign Object Damage	USMC	US Marine Corps
HOCF	Helicopter Operational Conversion Flight	WG	West Germany
		WGAF	West German Air Force
HSA	Hawker Siddeley Aviation	WHL	Westland Helicopters Ltd

Introduction

On 10 September 1912, 2-Lt E. Hotchkiss and Lt C. A. Bettington had the dubious distinction of being the first officers of the newly created Royal Flying Corps Reserves to be killed while engaged on military flying duties when their Bristol monoplane crashed on a flight from Salisbury Plain. The aircraft suffered a structural failure that caused the wing fabric to tear away and the aircraft to crash on the bank of the River Thames near Godstow in Oxfordshire. Within three weeks of the accident the flying of monoplanes by the Military Wing was banned by the Secretary of State for War with little more reason than that two wings were safer than one.

Ever since the Wright Brothers' first successful powered flight at Kittyhawk had taken place some nine years earlier, it was accepted that all flying would involve an element of risk. With the growth of military flying, which expanded at an unprecedented rate during World War 1, those risks multiplied as pilots and aircraft were flown to, and often beyond, their known limits.

However, with the end of hostilities in Europe, it became obvious that most of the casualties amongst pilots of the Royal Flying Corps (RFC) and Royal Naval Air Service (RNAS), and later the RAF, had been caused by flying accidents and only a minority had fallen to the enemy, and it was in response to an alarming number of these accidents that the Government of the day established the Accidents Investigation Branch (AIB) in 1919. The existence of the Branch was formalised with the Air Navigation Act of 1920, which required the Minister responsible for civil aviation to make regulations providing for the investigation of accidents arising during the course of air navigation within the UK, or to British-registered aircraft elsewhere in the world.

In its early days the AIB was a pseudo-military organisation concerned mainly with military aircraft accidents, for civil air transport at the time was very much in its infancy. In 1937, the AIB was placed under the auspices of the Director General of Aviation. However, with the advent of World War 2, there was a vast increase in the number of military accidents of which the AIB could only cover a mere 2%. This state of affairs prompted the member of the Air Force Board responsible for training to establish officers at Command Headquarters with responsibility to take preliminary investigating action to aid the AIB. While going some way to ease the load, it did not solve the problem completely and in 1942 the RAF became entirely responsible for investigating its own accidents.

The RAF's new flight safety organisation made dramatic inroads into accident prevention, although the remedial measures were noted by the Inspector General of the RAF as still haphazard, and the chain of flight safety responsibility was considered to be vague to say the least. It was not until 1944 that accident prevention was given Directorate status and staffed by an air commodore, two group captains, 20 wing commanders and a WRAF officer.

For some time during and immediately following World War 2, the Royal Navy claimed that, due to the very specialised nature of its flying activities, it should be allowed to create its own accident investigation organisation. In 1946 the Royal Naval Aircraft Accident Investigation Unit was established at Lee-on-Solent.

Although it suffered a drastic reduction of manpower during the postwar rundown of the armed services in the 1950s, the RAF Directorate of Flight Safety continued to be responsible for accident prevention, although not investigation as such. This was undertaken by Boards of Enquiry convened by the Command to which the aircraft involved belonged.

After World War 2, when civil aviation underwent a period of rapid expansion, the AIB was transferred to the Ministry of Civil Aviation, later the Department of Trade. Whilst being primarily concerned with civil aviation, the AIB provided technical support to the RAF Boards of Enquiry.

In 1957, an Army Air Corps (AAC) Flight Safety Officer joined the RAF Directorate of Flight Safety (which in 1977 became an Inspectorate), an arrangement that continued until 1980 when the Army established its own Flight Safety Centre at Middle Wallop. Since then it has convened its own Boards of Enquiry.

It has only been in the last two decades that military aircraft accidents, accident investigation procedures and accident prevention have become subjects openly discussed by the Government. Prior to this, but occasionally and somewhat reluctantly, the Government released extremely vague details of overall accident statistics and hardly ever published results of investigations. The authorities were often reluctant to acknowledge the fact that an accident had even occurred. However, in 1971,

this attitude changed, partly as a result of two military accidents that involved civilian casualties. Since 1977, Military Aircraft Accident Summaries (MAAS) of most British military accidents are made available to the press and yearly statistics are announced by the Minister of Defence in Parliament. This more open policy of information — although still less detailed than those made freely available in the United States and Scandinavia — has been of benefit to the Services who have been able to show that the incidence of military accidents, not counting the Falklands Campaign, has steadily declined over the past 20 years. However, military accidents, particularly those occurring within the British Isles, continue to make newspaper headlines and prompt calls by local MPs for a ban on low-level training flights. The fact that the British Services have withdrawn from most of their overseas bases during the last quarter of a century, and that the UK's overriding commitment in the 1980s is to NATO, means that the bulk of its air forces are based, and have to train, within the UK.

However, it is clear from the MoD's published data on accident investigation and prevention, that the services devote a large, and increasing, amount of time and resources to these vital areas. It is appreciated that with the continuing escalation in cost and complexity of the modern warplane, flight safety is of vital importance if a viable defence force is to be maintained with fewer aircraft than at any period since World War 2. It is equally important to establish with speed and certainty the cause of an accident when it does occur, in order to minimise the possibility of a repeat in the future.

Military Accident Investigation

At the present time Britain's three Services approach aircraft accident investigation in much the same way, although there are certain procedural differences.

Usually, the first report of an accident to an RAF aircraft is made to the Ministry of Defence (MoD) by the Flight Safety Officer of the station at which the aircraft is based, giving brief details such as the location, the extent of the damage caused and a report of any casualties resulting. If the accident is sufficiently serious, involving the loss of an aircraft or injuries to personnel, a Board of Inquiry will be convened by the owner Command.

The Board comprises of a President who is a senior officer — normally either a serving aircrew officer or recently current on the aircraft type involved, or with recent experience in its flying role. If for some reason the President does not have these qualifications, there will be a junior member of the Board who does. Also on the Board will be an engineering officer current on, or familiar with, the aircraft type. The Board will have access to specialist technical advice from the AIB at Farnborough and the Institute of Aviation Medicine and, if necessary, specialists from the aerospace industry.

The aim of the Board is not only to determine the cause as quickly as possible, but also to undertake an in-depth investigation which will establish the cause beyond any reasonable doubt. Although Presidents of Boards are required to send a signal 48-96hr after the accident to all interested parties, outlining their initial findings or making recommendations for immedi-ate action to be taken regarding a suspect component or operating procedure, it may take up to a year before the full Report is published. As with accidents of all types, flying accidents are often the result of a number of contributing factors. On average, however, the Board's report — which represents a comprehensive record of the accident with recommendations for subsequent action — is available within three months of the accident.

One of the most useful of the many organisations providing technical assistance to RAF Boards of Inquiry is the AIB which provides, on request, the services of an Engineering Inspector to advise the President on the wreckage analysis aspect of the investigation. Although the decision to ask for AIB assistance rests with the President of a Board of Inquiry, the AIB is normally asked to advise in cases of structural failures in the air, in-flight fires and accidents of an obscure nature.

Advances in design technology and materials knowledge in the production of modern fast jet aircraft have made structural failures in the air something of a rarity, although in recent years the Buccaneer and Phantom have suffered from such failures with catastrophic results. Once again, the latest generation of high-powered, high-technology engines have reduced the risk of in-flight fires although a number of older types still in service such as the Hunter, Lightning and Phantom, are prone to this type of accident.

Accidents of an Obscure Nature covers a wide spectrum, Birdstrikes and FOD (Foreign Object Damage) contribute to a number of accidents each year,

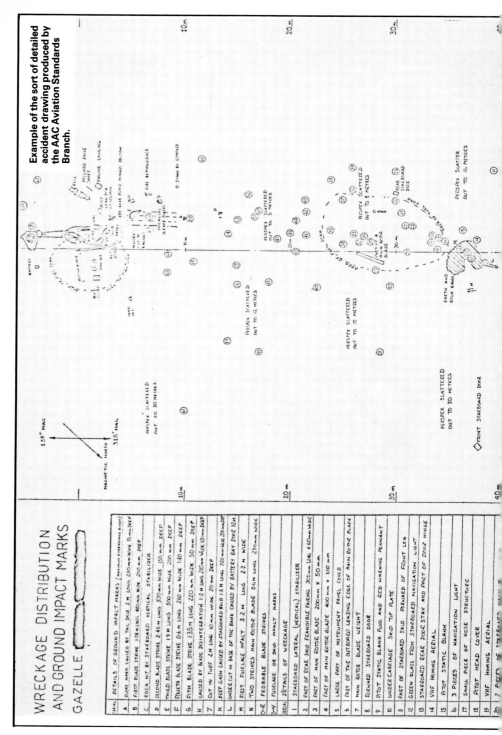

Example of the sort of detailed accident drawing produced by the AAC Aviation Standards Branch.

No.	Description
25	BLADE WEIGHT
26	PART OF PITOT TUBE
27	PART OF A MAIN ROTOR BLADE LEADING EDGE
28	PART OF PLYWOOD CABIN FLOOR COVERING RING
29	RADAR ALTIMETER AERIAL
30	PITOT DRAIN
31	PART OF THE NOSE STRUCTURE
32	PART OF BROKEN MAIN ROTOR HUB OIL RESERVOIR
33	PART OF BATTERY ACCESS PANEL
34	PART OF GLASS FIBRE BELLY PANEL
35	PART OF PTR 170 CONTROL BOX FACIA
36	BATTERY ACCESS PANEL / DOOR
37	FRACTURED BATTERY CONNECTOR LUG
38	ROTOR/COMPRESSOR NC GAUGE GLASS FACE COVER
39	PART OF CABIN HEAT DUCT
40	PART OF STARBOARD CENTRE STRUCTURE INCLUDING NAV LIGHT MOUNTING, EARTH SOCKET AND DOOR HINGE
41	PORT SLIDING WINDOW
42	BATTERY WEDGE
43	PORT DOOR UPPER SLIDING WINDOW RUNNER
44	STAND BY COMPASS CORRECTION CARD WITH MOUNTING AND STRUCTURE
45	PART OF CABIN FLOOR PLYWOOD COVERING
46	STABILIZED BINO SOCKET
47	PART OF CABIN FLOOR PLYWOOD COVERING AND SKID TIP TRIM
48	PORT SKID FORWARD OF FRONT LEG
49	TWO PIECES OF INSTRUMENT PANEL COVER
50	MIC TEL JACK PLUG BOX AND CYCLIC HANDGRIP TOGGLE SWITCH
51	VHF HOMING AERIAL
52	LARGE SECTION OF FLOOR AND LOWER SKIN PANEL AND PART OF BROKEN MAIN ROTOR HEAD RESERVOIR
53	PART OF PILOTS CYCLIC HAND GRIP
54	PART OF PILOTS CYCLIC HAND GRIP
55	BATTERY TRAY
56	HEAD SET LEAD INCLUDING SWITCH AND PLUG
57	MAI WEST WITH HARNESS CUT
58	LANDING LAMP FILAMENT AND PORTION OF REFLECTOR
59	COWLING STAY AND SEAT ADJUSTING KNOB
60	BLADE VERNIER SCALE
61	VERNIER POINTER
62	CENTRAL CABIN NOSE PILLAR
63	VHF HOMING AERIAL TUBE AND FITTING
64	LAMINATED COUPLING RING (FREEWHEEL TO MAIN GEAR BOX)
65	COWLING LATCH
66	PART OF THE FREEWHEEL FLANGE
67	MAIN ROTOR HUB OIL RESERVOIR AND VERNIER POINTER
68	GIMBAL RING PIN

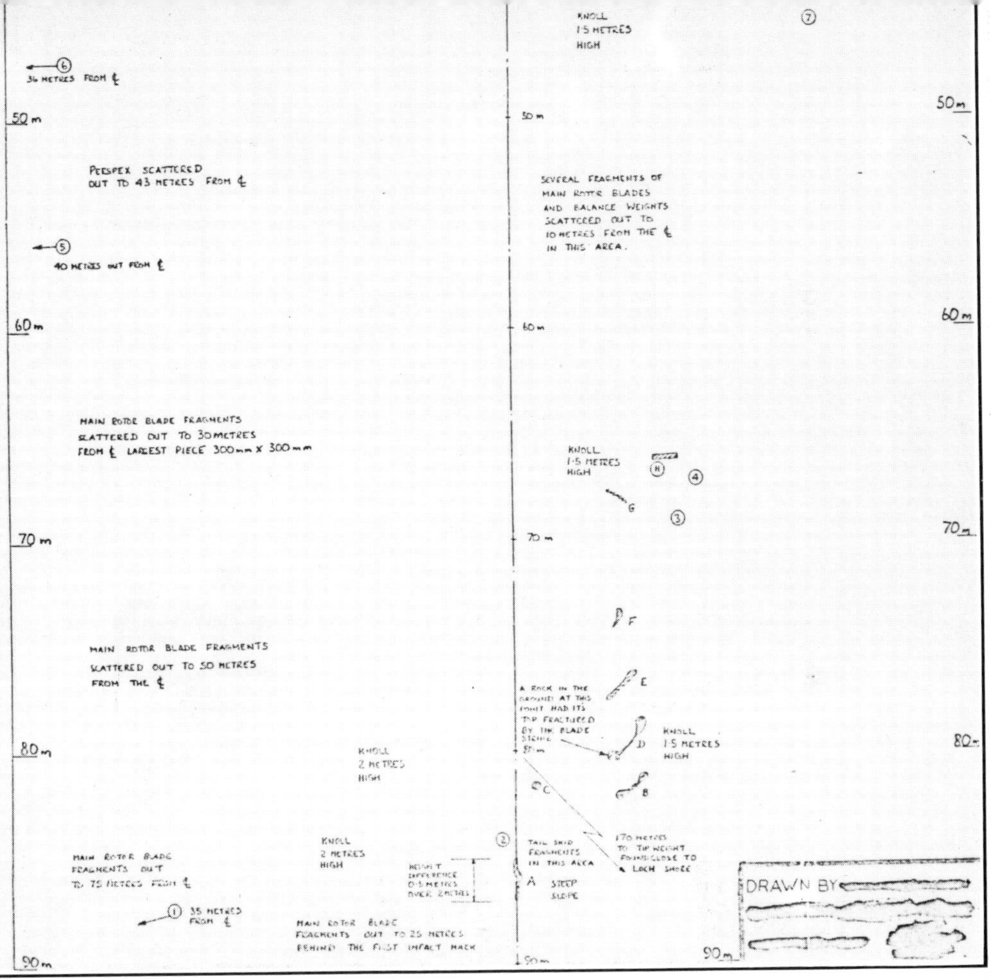

Diagram annotations (scale markers 50 m – 90 m):

KNOLL 15 METRES HIGH

SEVERAL FRAGMENTS OF MAIN ROTOR BLADES AND BALANCE WEIGHTS SCATTERED OUT TO 10 METRES FROM THE ℄ IN THIS AREA.

PERSPEX SCATTERED OUT TO 45 METRES FROM ℄

⑥ 36 METRES FROM ℄

⑤ 40 METRES OUT FROM ℄

MAIN ROTOR BLADE FRAGMENTS SCATTERED OUT TO 30 METRES FROM ℄ LARGEST PIECE 300mm x 300mm

KNOLL 15 METRES HIGH

MAIN ROTOR BLADE FRAGMENTS SCATTERED OUT TO 50 METRES FROM THE ℄

KNOLL 15 METRES HIGH

MAIN ROTOR BLADE FRAGMENTS OUT TO 25 METRES

KNOLL 2 METRES HIGH

① 35 METRES FROM ℄

MAIN ROTOR BLADE FRAGMENTS OUT TO 25 METRES FORMING THE FIRST IMPACT MARK

A ROCK IN THE GROUND AT THE FRONT HAD ITS TOP FRACTURED BY THE BLADE STRIKE

TAIL SKID FRAGMENTS IN THIS AREA

A STEEP SLOPE

170 METRES TO THE HEIGHT FRAMES CLOSE TO LOW RANGE

DRAWN BY

while human error remains statistically the largest cause of accidents in military aviation.

The human error factor is currently receiving more attention than at any previous time. Since 1983, RAF aircrew have been given psychological tests which are correlated with their progress through training. The Behavioural Scientist is frequently called to assist Boards of Inquiry and accidents that were often quickly dismissed as aircrew error are now seen to contain many contributory factors. The Accident Data Recorders now being fitted to some, but not all, the latest military aircraft should provide much needed evidence that will help to explain some of these accidents.

Flight Data Recorders (FDR) and Cockpit Voice Recorders (CVR) have been mandatory in civil passenger transport aircraft for some years now but it is only recently that they have been fitted to British military aircraft. However, only Hawk and Tornado aircraft currently have ADRs fitted and these greatly increase the available evidence in the event of an accident.

Most modern recorders use ¼in magnetic tape as a recording medium. The data recording is sequential over a 1sec time frame using a digital pulse code modulation system. Data recovery and analysis is rendered easier by computer-controlled playback equipment. The recorded data can be presented in many ways — digital listings and analogue traces used by the performance specialists, or as an instrument array on a Video Display Unit (VDU).

This recent development to the AIB Flight Data Recorder facility allows the investigating team to run through the flight, right up until the point of impact in real time, on a cockpit instrument display. The system will shortly be modified to incorporate the synchronised voice recording at the same console. The investigators will then be able both to see and hear the accident sequence developing.

Much of the AIB's investigations centre on wreckage analysis. As is the case for many military accidents — and particularly those where the structural break-up is severe — the wreckage may be removed from the accident site and transported to the AIB wreckage analysis facility at Farnborough. It is here that the detailed examination of the aircraft's structure and systems will be undertaken. A modern fast jet aircraft impacting the ground at high speed can penetrate up to a depth of 40ft. The structural damage will be such that the entire wreckage can only be removed from the site in several hundred large polythene bags.

The difficult task of recovering the wreckage of fixed-wing aircraft belonging to all three Services is undertaken by the RAF Field Repair Squadron based at RAF Abingdon. The unit has a team of specialists on 24hr call to go anywhere in the world (with the exception of West Germany where RAF Germany has its own salvage unit) at the request of a Board of Inquiry, usually working in close contact with an AIB Inspector. The team is headed by an assessor, usually an RAF Warrant Officer, who will grid the accident site before identifying and logging all visible pieces with their grid references. While this is being done, and before any of the wreckage is moved, photographs of the crash will be taken on the ground and often from the air by RAF Canberra PR9s. The Field Repair Squadron is responsible for making all systems safe — draining fuel tanks, removing live weapons and ammunition, gas and oxygen cylinders, releasing pressure in hydraulic systems and high-pressure tyres that can explode some time after impact if damaged in the crash or by fire. The latter are often punctured by rifle fire before being removed. Electrical fires deep within the wreckage will burn for some considerable time after impact and have to be dealt with as soon as possible.

When the AIB Inspectors have finished their on-site investigations, the unit begins to collect small pieces of wreckage in polythene bags while larger pieces are retrieved with the use of specialised vehicles, usually belonging to the Royal Engineers in the UK, or local private plant contractors in other countries. Thankfully, military aircraft accidents usually occur in remote areas, often on high ground, and this calls for the use of specialised all-terrain vehicles for recovery of the wreckage. If the wreckage has to be cut up into smaller components to facilitate its removal, all cuts have to be clearly marked by the salvage team. When all accessible wreckage has been removed it is weighed to ascertain how much of the total aircraft has been recovered. The team will use metal detectors over the site if they consider that vital parts have been missed. The Repair Squadron will supervise the removal of all contaminated soil from the crash site, resulting from the spillage of fuel, hydraulic fluid etc, and its replacement with new soil. The matter of liability for the damage to property is also handled by the Squadron, but costs arising from that liability are settled by the MoD.

Depending on the extent of the damage, the wreckage will be transported to the AIB at Farnborough or returned to the aircraft's owner unit. If the accident occurs abroad, or if the cost of recovery to the UK is unwarranted, the Repair Squadron will sometimes sell the wreckage to local scrap dealers.

At Farnborough the daunting task of separating the wreckage into the various aircraft systems begins. This phase of the technical investigation is very labour-intensive and necessarily painstaking. Although no-one involved wants to go through this exercise more than once in the investigation, invariably a second sift is necessary, often looking for fragments of a specific component. After the systems have been removed, detailed examination can begin. The objective is to be able to establish the integrity or otherwise of each system at impact and to determine control positions both in the cockpit and at each control surface. Most of the evidence comes from impact marking. However, even without the help of an ADR it is often possible to establish events that took place whilst the aircraft was still in flight, knowing the response time and sequencing of a system. High-speed impacts have the effect of freezing certain components in their immediate pre-impact positions. It is on these components that the investigators concentrate in order to establish the possible status/position throughout the system. If the system was functioning normally then these indications should give a good correlation. If this is not evident it may suggest a systems failure or malfunction before impact. Every component is subjected to radiographic examination before functional testing, or strip examination. The detailed examination will be carried out with the knowledge that a hasty or wrong move could destroy vital evidence.

After the investigation is complete and the Board of Inquiry has published its Accident Report, the wreckage is sold for scrap. From time to time larger components, such as a wing, will be passed to the RAF Battlefield Damage Flight, also based at RAF Abingdon, for assessment of its strength and ability to withstand severe impact damage.

The RAF Inspectorate of Flight Safety is staffed by 15 officers from the aircrew and engineering branches covering 36 types of aircraft and collates all available information of incidents and accidents in order to advise the service, at all levels, on all aspects of flight safety. Information from Boards of Inquiry, station Flight Safety Officers and individual servicemen are studied and analysed and cross-checked for any similarities with previous accident reports, the results of which are passed on to all interested parties both within the Service, and to the RN or AAC if a common type is involved.

The Inspectorate publishes a regular flight safety feature in the RAF magazine *Air Clues* under the *nom de plume* Wg Cdr Spry in which aircrew are encouraged to write, anonymously, about any 'near-misses' that they may have experienced. In addition to the more formal reporting, the Inspectorate has a confidential direct reporting system, called CONDOR, that is available to aircrew, air traffic controllers or anyone involved in the operations of aircraft in the air. A similar system for engineers is called MURPHY!

Regular two-day courses are held for station Flight Safety Officers which are backed up by formal visits to units by the Inspectorate's officers. Informal and unannounced visits are also made to units in order to listen to anyone who wants to talk about flight safety-related subjects, often in the relaxed atmosphere of the Mess bar.

In addition to the UK military sources of flight safety information, the Inspectorate is represented on the predominantly civilian UK Flight Safety Committee, and on other joint committees either directly related to, or having influence on, flight safety. It also exchanges information with the safety organisations of the majority of European air forces and United States Air Forces Europe (USAFE) all of which belong to a NATO Committee which has the Inspector of Flight Safety for the RAF as its Chairman.

The Inspectorate can formulate concepts for flight safety and pass on recommendations for new equipment to ACAS, such as retrofitting of ADRs to all RAF helicopters or the review of training procedures.

The AAC's own Aviation Standards Branch is based broadly on the RAF organisation; RAF Boards of Inquiry investigated AAC accidents until 1971.

Since establishing its own accident investigation organisation in 1946, the Royal Navy has developed a two-way inquiry system. The Navy convenes a Board of Inquiry for all accidents, presided over by a Commander or Lieutenant-Commander (Aviation), comprising of an engineering officer and a doctor. The purpose of the Board is to issue a report within two weeks of the accident. In the event of a major, Cat 4 or 5 accident, the Royal Navy's Aircraft Accident Investigation Unit (AAIU) begins its own in-depth technical investigation concurrently with the Board of Inquiry.

The AAIU/based at RNAS Lee-on-Solent is staffed by four Officer Engineers and four Petty Officer Specialists under the command of a Lieutenant-Commander (Air). A three-man team of AAIU investigators is held on 24hr alert, ready to travel anywhere in the UK and Europe in the event of a serious accident, where they plot and record the wreckage for up to two days before it is moved. Another 10 days will be spent identifying pieces of wreckage before it is turned over to the RAF Field Repair Squadron if a fixed-wing aircraft is involved, or the Royal Navy's own Transport and Repair Unit if it is a rotary-wing aircraft, when it will be transported to one of the three AAIU hangars at Lee-on-Solent for detailed examination. The Unit is capable of the detailed technical analysis of the wreckage that the AIB undertakes at Farnborough for the RAF and AAC.

The Royal Navy is also responsible for the salvage of all wreckage from the sea and has a small fleet of specialist craft dedicated to the retrieval of aircraft that crash into the water around the British Isles. Commercial salvage companies are also on call when required and up to six months will be spent searching for a particular aircraft, especially if it is a new type in service. The difficulties which surround these salvage operations are compounded if the wreckage is from a fast jet aircraft, because they tend to disintegrate on impact with the sea and strong tidal currents around the British Isles spread the wreckage over a wide area. The North Sea, which is where most fast jet

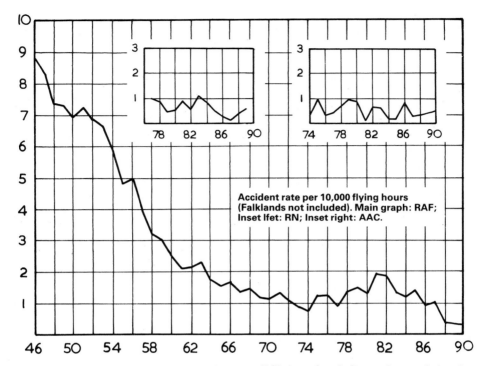

Accident rate per 10,000 flying hours (Falklands not included). Main graph: RAF; Inset lfet: RN; Inset right: AAC.

salvage operations tend to occur, is a difficult area to search because of poor underwater visibility. However, most modern fast jets are fitted with sonar locator beacons which are designed to activate when immersed in water and so pinpoint an aircraft when it crashes into the sea. Helicopters tend not to disintegrate to the same degree and the bulk of the wreckage is often held together by the electrical wiring looms, fuel and hydraulic lines, and the control lines.

A final AAIU report on a major accident will take up to a year to prepare. Over the last six years it has been able to establish the cause of accidents with sufficient authority to make worthwhile recommendations to prevent recurrence in 91% of those into which it has carried out full investigation. The Royal Navy Flight Safety Centre, established in 1962 at Yeovilton, is responsible for implementing these recommendations as well as collating all flight safety information and circulating it to all units within the Services, as well as training Flight Safety Officers wherever Royal Navy aircraft are operated, be it an airfield or a ship.

The flight safety organisations of all three Services are looking to the immediate future and addressing themselves to the increasingly complex problems of: disorientation of pilots of fast jets with large canopies and low sills; G-loc (G-induced loss of consciousness); the increasing use of composite materials; glass cockpits; fly-by-wire controls; and the growing dependence on micro-chip technology in the modern military aircraft.

However, despite the complex high-technology construction of the modern warplane, the most important factor in military flight safety remains much the same as it did when the first fatal aircraft crash occurred in 1908 — the human factor.

British Military Aircraft Accident Log 1966-90

1966

Date	Type	Serial	Unit	Location	Cause
05/01	Lightning F3	XR721	56 Sqn	Helmington, Suffolk	Belly landing in field following engine failure; DBR
02/02	Canberra PR7	WT531	80 Sqn	Nr Berriedale, Scotland	Flew into high ground
02/02	Sioux AH1	XT187	ACC	Nr Stockbridge, Hants	Crashed in field
09/02	Sea Vixen FAW1	XJ567	766 Sqn	Cadbury, Somerset	Crashed following instrument failure at night
10/02	Jet Provost T4	XS221	20 Sqn	Alor Star, Malaya	Hit trees and crashed during FAC trials
11/02	Vulcan B2	XH536	12 Sqn	Nr Swansea	Low-level
28/02	Sycamore HR14	XL826	CFS	RAF Ternhill	Roll over on landing
03/03	Lightning F3	XP699	56 Sqn	Nr Wethersfield, Yorks	Abandoned following fire warning; Ej
15/03	Lightning F1A	XM190	226 OCU	RAF Coltishall	Abandoned following engine fire; Ej
17/03	Sea Vixen FAW2	XS581	893 Sqn	10nm off Portland	Crashed into sea at night; 2F
22/03	Sea Vixen FAW2	XN701	890 Sqn	Nr Singapore	Crashed into sea following premature explosion of practice bombs; 2F
24/03	Sea Vixen FAW1	XJ522	766 Sqn	Moreton Hampstead, Devon	Mid-air collision with another Sea Vixen which landed safely; 2F
25/03	Buccaneer S1	XN970	800 Sqn	Indian Ocean off Beira	Crashed into sea while operating from HMS *Eagle*; 2F
28/03	Buccaneer S1	XN950	750 Sqn	Lossiemouth	Crashed during overshoot; Ej; 1F
04/04	Canberra B15	XK641	45 Sqn	Pahang, Malaya	Dived into high ground following loss of control; 3F
04/04	Javelin FAW9	XH785	60 Sqn	Nr Tengah, Malaya	Abandoned following engine explosion; Ej
13/04	Gnat T1	XP507	4FTS	RAF Valley	Crashed into sea on approach
18/04	Vulcan B2	XH556	230 OCU	RAF Finningley	Ground fire
26/04	Javelin FAW9	XH717	60 Sqn	Butterworth, Malaya	Start-up fire, DBR
03/05	Canberra B2	WH857	97 Sqn	RAF Watton	Stalled on overshoot following misjudged asymmetric approach; 3F
04/05	Jet Provost T4	XP670	7FTS	Nr Coxwold, Yorks	Abandoned following loss of control in spin
04/05	Hastings C1	TG575	–	El Adem, Libya	–
06/05	Lightning F1A	XM213	226 OCU	RAF Coltishall	Undercarriage retraction during take-off run

16

10/05	Gannet AEW3	XL475	849 Sqn	Off Okinawa, Japan	Ditched in sea following loss of nose wheel during launch from HMS *Ark Royal*
10/05	Sea Vixen FAW1	XJ520	890 Sqn	HMS *Ark Royal*, Beira Straits	Crashed into sea following engine failure during blockade patrol; Ej; 1F
13/05	Gnat T1	XR539	4FTS	Nr Gwynedd, Wales	Spun into ground; Ej
16/05	Scout AH1	XR634	3 Wing	Aden	Crashed in open ground
23/05	Gnat T1	XR570	4FTS	Nr Mona, Anglesey	Hit HT cables
26/05	Jet Provost T3	XM384	2FTS	Woodborough, Leics	Mid-air collision with XP631 during formation aerobatics; Ej
26/05	Jet Provost T4	XP631	2FTS	Woodborough, Leics	Mid-air collision
02/06	Whirlwind HAR10	XP342	CFS	Nr Llangollen, Denbigh	Wirestrike at 70ft in valley
05/06	Canberra B(1)8	XM270	16 Sqn	RAF Gutersloh, WG	Spun into ground on approach
09/06	Buccaneer S2	XN979	801 Sqn	HMS *Victorious*, off the Lizard	Crashed in sea after launch; Ej
14/06	Wessex HAS1	XM832	815 Sqn	Southampton Water	Ditched in sea following power failure

Date	Type	Serial	Unit	Location	Remarks
14/06	Javelin FAW9	XH709	64 Sqn	Nr New Skudai Estate, Malaya	–; Ej
14/06	Varsity T1	WF334	BCBS	Nr Immingham	Destroyed in force-landing following mid-air collision with Cessna 337A
15/06	Sea Vixen FAW2	XS584	893 Sqn	HMS *Eagle*, Off Hartland Point	Crashed into sea
16/06	Hunter F6	XG157	234 Sqn	Nr Challacombe, Devon	Crashed into high ground emerging from low cloud; 1F
17/06	Wessex HAS1	XM921	706 Sqn	RNAS Culdrose	Crashed after being hit by Whirlwind XM686 while hovering at Predannack
17/06	Whirlwind HAS7	XM921	705 Sqn	RNAS Culdrose	Crashed after hitting Wessex XM686 during take-off from Predannack
21/06	Sioux AH1	XT129	AAC Centre	Nr Baverstock, Wilts	Crashed and burnt out after hitting power lines
22/06	Canberra B15	WH927	32 Sqn	2nm N Wheelus, Libya	Abandoned following wing root explosion; 3Ej
23/06	Chipmunk T10	WK631	Birmingham UAS	Tibberton Grange, Shropshire	Mid-air collision with WP834
23/06	Chipmunk T10	WP834	Birmingham UAS	Tibberton Grange, Shropshire	Mid-air collision
24/06	Gannet AEW3	XL493	849 Sqn	Off Singapore	Crashed into sea during training flight from HMS *Eagle*
29/06	Victor SR2	XM716	543 Sqn	RAF Wyton	Broke up during high-speed low-level run; 4F
30/06	Buccaneer S1	XK528	RAE	West Freugh	Exploded in mid-air and crashed into the sea
01/07	Lightning T5	XS453	226 OCU	Nr Hapisburgh, Norfolk	Abandoned following jammed undercarriage; Ej
08/07	Sea Vixen FAW2	XP958	899 Sqn	Changi, Malaya	Crashed on night approach; 2F
11/07	Sioux AH1	XT136	ARWF	Nr Whitchurch, Hants	Crashed following engine failure
12/07	Auster AOP9	WZ722	38 Gp Comms Flt	Odiham	Stalled and crashed on take-off
20/07	Wessex HAS1	XP114	706 Sqn	Culdrose	Crashed on approach following power failure
27/07	Jet Provost T3	XP625	CAW	North Frodingham	Abandoned at low level following birdstrike
27/07	Lightning F3	XR714	111 Sqn	RAF Akrotiri, Cyprus	Undercarriage retracted on take-off; DBR
29/07	Chipmunk T10	WD377	12 AEF	Nr Lochindorb, Morayshire	Crashed during force-landing
30/07	Sioux AH1	XT216	4 Wing	Kuching, Malaysia	Crashed in open ground
05/08	Sea Vixen FAW2	XS586	893 Sqn	49nm from Gan	Ditched in sea following fuel loss
08/08	Buccaneer S1	XN949	736 Sqn	Moray Firth	Crashed into sea; 2F
24/08	Lightning F3	XP760	23 Sqn	Nr Seahouses, Fife	Abandoned following engine failure; Ej

Date	Type	Serial	Unit	Location	Cause
25/08	Javelin FAW9	XH876	64 Sqn	Tengah, Malaya	Abandoned on approach; Ej
14/09	Jet Provost T4	XP616	1FTS	Nr Helmsley	Flew into high ground in bad weather
15/09	Sea Vixen FAW2	XJ606	893 Sqn	Off Cubi Point, Philippines	Ditched in sea during training flight from HMS *Victorious*
28/09	Gnat T1	XM704	CFS	RAF Kemble	Crashed on take-off
04/10	Jet Provost T4	XR645	7FTS	Nr Church Fenton	Dived into ground
04/10	Wasp HAS1	XT425	829 Sqn	10nm off Portland	Ditched in sea during night exercise
06/10	Buccaneer S2	XV153	801 Sqn	Subic Bay, Philippines	Stalled on take-off during stores configuration tests
21/10	Javelin FAW9	XH958	228 OCU	RAF Leeming	Crashed on approach
06/12	Chipmunk T10	WZ864	Southampton Hamble UAS	Mid-air collision on approach with Chipmunk G-ATEA
06/12	Sioux AH1	XT125	1 Rgt	Camau Peninsula, Aden	Crashed in desert; 2F
14/12	Javelin FAW9	XH848	29 Sqn	RAF Akrotiri, Cyprus	Abandoned on approach; Ej
21/12	Beaver AL1	XP770	132 Flt	Nr Salisbury, Hants	Crashed into trees
30/12	Hunter FGA9	XE646	1 Sqn	RAF Leconfield	Abandoned during approach following engine failure; Ej
30/12	Jet Provost T4	XP569	2FTS	Nr East Drayton, Notts	Spun into ground

1967

Date	Type	Serial	Unit	Location	Cause
02/01	Lightning T4	XM971	226 OCU	RAF Coltishall	Abandoned following radar fairing coming loose on approach; Ej
02/01	Wasp HAS1	XT414	829 Sqn	Irish Sea	Ditched following gearbox failure
18/01	Javelin FAW9	XH800	29 Sqn	RAF Akrotiri, Cyprus	Crashed on approach
23/01	Sea Vixen FAW1	XJ564	892 Sqn	Mediterranean	Crashed into sea off Gibraltar following lauch from HMS *Hermes*
23/01	Wessex HAS1	XS883	826 Sqn	Off Gibraltar	Collided with bows of MHS *Hermes* during rescue of Sea Vixen XJ564 crew
23/01	Hunter FR10	WW595	4 Sqn	Nr Furstenburg, WG	Flew into high ground; 1F
20/02	Hunter FGA9	XF414	20 Sqn	Nr Layang, Malaya	Abandoned following power loss; Ej

HRH Prince Philip was the first member of the Royal Family to fly in a helicopter when he flew several sorties in a civil Dragonfly belonging to the manufacturer Westland on an official visit to Germany in March 1953. Although the King's Flight had used helicopters to fly mail to and from Balmoral as long ago as 1947 using Sikorsky Hoverfly Mk 1s, it was not until September 1954 that the Flight, now the Queen's, received its first VVIP-modified helicopter, a Westland Dragonfly HC4, on extended loan from the Central Flying School Helicopter Unit. Four years later, a contract for two VVIP Whirlwinds was placed with Westland. However, numerous changes in engine specifications delayed the delivery of these aircraft until May 1964 when the first of two VVIP Whirlwind HCC12 versions of the Gnome-engined HAR10, XR487, was finally handed over to the Queen's Flight at RAF Benson.

After three years of trouble-free service and while *en route* to Yeovil on 7 December 1967, where a meeting was to be held to discuss its successor, the VVIP Wessex, Whirlwind XR487 crashed at Brightwalton, Berks, following the failure of the main rotor shaft. The weather had been very cold but clear and the accident had been witnessed by a number of people on the ground. One of them told what he saw: 'Suddenly a rotor blade flew off like a spinning top and the helicopter nose-dived into the ground and exploded in flames.'

Although villagers were quickly on the scene, all four occupants on board the Royal Whirlwind, Air Cdre J. H. L. Blount DFC, the Captain of the Queen's Flight since 2 August 1964, Sqn Ldr M. W. Hermon, the Flight's Engineering Officer since 9 September 1967, the pilot, Sqn Ldr J. H. Liversedge, and the navigator, Flt Lt R. Fisher, were killed in the crash and the helicopter totally destroyed.

All Whirlwind helicopters throughout the services were immediately grounded pending the report of the Board of Inquiry into the accident, including the Queen's Flight's second Whirlwind, XR486, which at the time of the accident had been flying the Duke of Edinburgh during a tour of Germany. The Flight was not to fly another Royal Helicopter sortie until March 1968. However, the type was again grounded in 1969 following an accident to a standard RAF Whirlwind HAR10 and the Queen's Flight HCC12s were replaced by Wessex HCC4s in July 1969. These aircraft are still in service in 1990 with no obvious successor in sight.

Standard RAF Whirlwind HAR10. *Dane Allport*

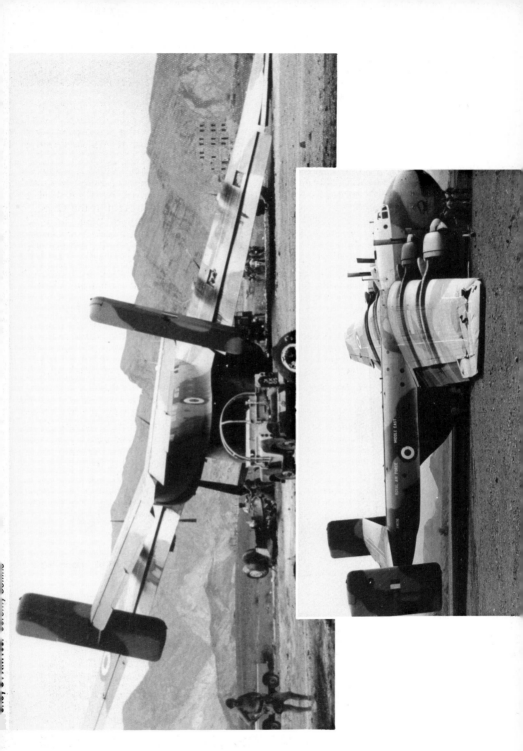

Date	Type	Serial	Unit	Location	Remarks
20/02	Hunter FGA9	XF440	8/43 Sqn	Al Ittihad, Qater	Abandoned following in-flight fire; Ej
22/02	Hunter GA11	WT805	738 Sqn	St Brides Bay, Wales	Crashed into sea on approach to Brawdy
23/02	Canberra B(I)6	WT322	213 Sqn	Wesseke, WG	Dived into ground following loss of control at low level over the Nordhorn range; 2F
01/03	Sioux AH1	XT798	CFS	RAF Ternhill	Crashed and burnt out
03/03	Lightning F3	XP699	56 Sqn	Wethersfield	Crashed following fuel line failure
23/03	Hunter FGA9	XF421	8/43 Sqn	Khormaksar, Aden	Overshot into sea following power-off landing
01/04	Whirlwind HAR10	XL111	Aden SAR Flt	Khormaksar, Aden	Crashed following engine failure
06/04	Vulcan B2	XL385	27 Sqn	RAF Scampton	Engine explosion on take-off. Burnt on ground
17/04	Lightning F1A	XM184	226 OCU	RAF Coltishall	Fire on landing
17/04	Canberra T4	WT489	231 OCU	Steeple Morden, Cambs	Crashed into house on approach to RAF Bassingbourn; 2F
18/04	Hunter F6	XG273	54 Sqn	El Adem, Libya	Mid-air collision on approach; Ej
18/04	Hunter F6	XF446	54 Sqn	El Adem, Libya	Mid-air collision
27/04	Hunter FGA9	XJ691	208 Sqn	18nm SE Bahrain	Crashed into sea off Muharraq
28/04	Twin Pioneer C1	XN321	209 Sqn	Butterworth, Malaya	Engine failure during take-off
06/05	Hunter FGA9	XE532	92 Sqn	–	–
09/05	Canberra B(I)8	XH204	3 Sqn	Nr Wesel, WG	Abandoned following jammed aileron; Ej
15/05	Hunter F6	XG200	229 OCU	Tintagel, Cornwall	Abandoned following mid-air collision; Ej
15/05	Hunter F6	XG235	229 OCU	Tintagel, Cornwall	Abandoned following mid-air collision; Ej
18/05	Jet Provost T3	XN588	1FTS	Nr Wharren-le-Street, Yorks	Dived into ground
30/05	Javelin FAW9	XH708	64 Sqn	Nr Tengah, Malaya	Mid-air collision; F
30/05	Javelin FAW9	XH896	64 Sqn	Nr Tengah, Malaya	Mid-air collision; Ej
05/06	Devon C1	VP966	Embassy Flt	Amman, Jordan	Burnt out on the ground following Israeli air attack
21/06	Beverley C1	XM106	84 Sqn	Habulaia, Aden	Hit mine on runway
22/06	Whirlwind HAR10	XJ414	202 Sqn	Off Gt Yarmouth	Broke-up in mid-air and crashed into the sea following main rotor failure
23/06	Sioux AH1	XT173	3 Wing	Crater, Aden	Shot down by ground fire
29/06	Canberra T4	WD963	45 Sqn	2nm S of Tengah, Singapore	Abandoned over sea following double engine failure; Ej
30/06	Gnat T1	XM707	CFS	2½nm WNW Kemble	Abandoned after loss of pitch control; Ej
19/07	Hunter T8	XF978	764 Sqn	Moray Firth	Crashed into sea

Date	Type	Serial	Unit	Location	Remarks
03/08	Hunter F6	XF443	229 OCU	1nm SE of Chivenor	Crashed into railway cutting during emergency approach following engine failure
07/08	Whirlwind HAR10	XP460	230 Sqn	RAF Odiham	Heavy power-off practice landing; DBR
09/08	Wessex HAS1	XS879	826 Sqn	Subic Bay, Phillipines	Ditched in sea
17/08	Chipmunk T10	WB558	Old Sarum Flt		Crashed following mid-air collision with glider
23/08	Gnat T1	XP512	4FTS	Rhosneigr, Anglesey	Abandoned over sea following hydraulic failure; Ej
04/09	Hunter F6	XG198	229 OCU	Ferry Side, Carmarthen	Dived into ground during practice attack on Pembrey Range; 1F
07/09	Scout AH1	XT641	13 Flt	Little Aden	Lost tail rotor after being hit by ground fire
07/09	Lightning F6	XR766	23 Sqn	51nm ENE Leuchars	Abandoned over sea in spin; Ej
12/09	Chipmunk T10	WK610	Bristol UAS	2nm SW Portishead, Somerset	Abandoned following mid-air collision
12/09	Chipmunk T10	WP838	Bristol UAS	2nm SW Portishead, Somerset	Abandoned following mid-air collision
13/09	Lightning F1	XM136	WatTFF	RAF Coltishall	Engine failure on approach
14/09	Twin Pioneer C1	XM959	152 Sqn	Tajibah, Oman	Crashed on landing
27/09	Lightning F3	XR714	111 Sqn	–	Crashed on landing
11/10	Javelin FAW9	XH788	60 Sqn	Nr Tengah, Malaya	Broke-up in the air
12/10	Britannia C1	XL638	511 Sqn	Khormaksar, Aden	Crashed on overshoot
18/10	Wessex HU5	XT457	845 Sqn	Glen Airstrip, Rockingham, USA	Crashed on take-off following power failure
27/10	Whirlwind HAR10	XK990	202 Sqn	RAF Acklington	Crashed during practice forced landing following engine failure
4/11	Shackleton MR2	WL786	205 Sqn	Indian Ocean	Crashed into sea en route for Changi following engine failure and wing fire; 8F
13/11	Wessex HAS1	XS864	829 Sqn	Off Portland	Ditched and sank in sea following engine failure
19/11	Shackleton MR3	WR976	201 Sqn	200nm off Cornish Coast	Hit sea during low-level turn; 9F
20/11	Hunter FGA9	XE654	8 Sqn	Oman	Flew into ground during practice ground attack
22/11	Sea Venom FAW21	XG699	750 Sqn	Lossiemouth	Crashed on overshoot
04/12	Sea Vixen FAW2	XJ558	RNAS Belfast	Irish sea	Flew into sea during test flight; 2F
07/12	Whirlwind HCC12	XR481	Queen's Flt	Brightwalton, Berks	Crashed following main rotor failure; 4F
14/12	Gnat T1	XP509	4FTS	RAF Valley	Belly landing
15/12	Beverley C1	XL150	34 Sqn	60nm N Seletar, Malaya	Crashed into high ground in bad weather; 6F

15/12	Hunter T8	XF322	738 Sqn	St George's Channel, 20nm SW of Brawdy	Crashed into sea following mid-air collision with Hunter XF938
15/12	Hunter T8	XF938	759 Sqn	St George's Channel, 20nm SW of Brawdy	Crashed into sea following mid-air collision with XF322
21/12	Shackleton MR3	XF702	206 Sqn	Nr Inverness	Dived into ground in extreme weather conditions; 11F

1968

Date	Type	Serial	Unit	Location	Cause
24/01	Lightning F6	XS900	5 Sqn	Nr Lossiemouth	Abandoned following jammed controls; Ej
26/01	Hunter T8	XL582	Heron Flt	Yeovilton	Abandoned following engine failure on take-off; Ej
30/01	Vulcan B2	XM604	9 Sqn	RAF Cottesmore	Engine fire on approach
30/01	Scout AH1	XT625	11 Flt	Nr Gerik, Malaya	Crashed following engine failure
02/02	Scout AH1	XT615	1 Flt	Nr Sharjah	Crashed following engine failure
05/02	Javelin	?	80 Sqn	RAF Seletar, Malaya	Undercarriage collapsed on landing
06/02	Sioux AH1	XT150	6 Flt	Malaya	Crashed in jungle
16/02	Sea Vixen FAW2	XJ516	893 Sqn	Yeovilton	Abandoned following loss of control on approach; Ej
21/02	Jet Provost T4	XP561	1FTS	RAF Linton	Abandoned following loss of control in cloud; Ej
26/02	Jet Provost T4	XP675	CFS	Nr Hanling, Glos	Mid-air collision with XP229; DBR
26/02	Jet Provost T4	XS229	CFS	Nr Hanling, Glos	Mid-air collision; Ej
05/03	Whirlwind HAS7	XL884	Stn Flt	Lossiemouth	Crashed on approach following power loss
11/03	Canberra B16	WJ770	6 Sqn	Calbria, Italy	Hit mountain; 3F
23/03	Hunter T8	XE664	764 Sqn	Nr Lossiemouth	Crashed on approach following flameout; Ej; 1F
31/03	Sioux AH1	XT565	17 Flt	West Germany	Crashed into high ground
04/04	Wessex HU5	XS494	–	Sembewang, Malaya	Rolled over on lift-off
08/04	Wessex HAS1	XP115	737 Sqn	English Channel	Ditched in sea during sortie from HMS Kent
17/04	Wasp HAS1	XS540	829 Sqn	Off Cape Point, South Africa	Crashed into sea while operating off HMS Aurora
19/04	Shackleton MR2	WB833	210 Sqn	Clyde Estuary	Hit high ground on the Mull of Kintyre; 11F

25/04	Wessex HC2	XT677	18 Sqn	Rheinsehlen Camp, WG	Flew into ground in fog at night on approach
29/04	Lightning F6	XS924	5 Sqn	Nr Beelsby, Lincs	Dived into ground following loss of control during flight refuelling; 1F
02/05	Chipmunk T10	WZ874	CFS	Nr Moreton-in-Marsh, Glos	Spun into ground
06/05	Hunter FGA9	XE532	208 Sqn	3nm WSW Dubai	Abandoned over the Persian Gulf following hitting radio mast on range during rocket firing sortie; Ej
07/05	Argosy C1	XR133	267 Sqn	Got-el-Afraq airstrip, Libya	Crashed during low-level run; F
17/05	Whirlwind HAS7	XL878	705 Sqn	Off Weymouth Pier	Ditched in sea following engine failure
20/05	Buccaneer S2	XV158	736 Sqn	Moray Firth	Crashed into sea

Date	Type	Serial	Unit	Location	Remarks
08/06	Gnat T1	XR999	4FTS	N Wales	Abandoned over sea following jammed controls; Ej
11/06	Canberra B(I)6	WT363	14 Sqn	Annendaal, Holland	Mid-air collision near Brüggen
18/06	Whirlwind HAR10	XS412	230 Sqn	Nr Basingstoke Hants	Forced landing in wood following engine failure; DBR
26/06	Hunter FGA9	XF388	8 Sqn	50nm SE Dubai	Abandoned over the desert following engine seisure; Ej
01/07	Buccaneer S2	XV335	736 Sqn	Nr Pt of Stoer, Sunderland	Crashed into sea
15/07	Hunter T7	WV253	ETPS	Lyme Bay nr Eype	Crashed into sea following failure to recover from intentional spin
22/07	Hunter FGA9	XJ674	20 Sqn	1nm S Tengah, Singapore	Abandoned following hydraulic failure; Ej
24/07	Sea Vixen FAW2	XJ489	899 Sqn	Chivenor	Crashed in finals; 2F
12/08	Sioux AH1	XT809	HQ 2 Wing	Libya	Crashed in dust cloud on take-off
15/08	Chipmunk T10	WG483	AAC	2nm SW Middle Wallop	Hit HT cables following loss of power
19/08	Victor K1A	XH646	TTF	Nr Kelling Heath, Norfolk	Mid-air collision; F
19/08	Canberra B(I)6	WT325	213 Sqn	Nr Kelling Heath, Norfolk	Mid-air collision; F
12/09	Lightning F6	XS896	74 Sqn	4nm NE Tengah, Malaya	Spun into ground following fire on approach
16/09	Wessex HAS1	XS124	820 Sqn	Atlantic	Ditched in sea off HMS *Eagle*
17/09	Wasp HAS1	XT440	829 Sqn	North Sea	Ditched in sea off Dutch coast while operating from HMS *Cleopatra*
31/10	Wessex HAS1	XS865	820 Sqn	English Channel	Ditched following power loss
05/11	Whirlwind HAR10	XR456	103 Sqn	7nm W Mersing, Malaya	Force-landing following engine failure; DBR
06/11	Hunter T8	XF942	759 Sqn	Off Brawdy	Crashed into sea during aerobatic practice
14/11	Gnat T1	XP510	4FTS	Nr Nevin, Caern	Abandoned over Irish Sea following loss of control in dive; Ej
15/11	Wasp HAS1	XS533	829 Sqn	Lyme Bay	Ditched in sea off HMS *Yarmouth*
21/11	Whirlwind HAS7	XM687	771 Sqn	Off Weymouth	Crashed into sea following loss of tail cone
22/11	Gannet AEW3	XL451	849 Sqn	Off Okinawa, Japan	Crashed into the sea while operating from HMS *Hermes*
25/11	Gannet AEW3	XL455	849 Sqn	Off Okinawa, Japan	Crashed into sea followng launch from HMS *Hermes*
29/11	Lightning F1A	XM174	Leu UAS	Nr Leuchars	Abandoned following engine fire; Ej
30/11	Chipmunk T10	WB573	Southampton UAS	Dunkery Beacon, Somerset	Flew into high ground during bad weather
18/12	Sea Vixen FAW2	XN657	893 Sqn	Changi, Singapore	Hit sea on night approach

Date	Type	Serial	Unit	Location	Cause
07/01	Canberra PR9	XH164	13 Sqn	RAF Luqa, Malta	Crashed on approach; 2F
09/01	Sea Vixen FAW2	XJ559	766 Sqn	Nr Ilchester	Crashed during single engine approach to Yeovilton
15/01	Gannet AEW3	XL452	849 Sqn	South Wales	Crashed into sea
15/01	Sea King HAS1	XV372	Rolls-Royce	West Harptree, Somerset	Crashed in bad weather following the failure of both engines due to ice ingestion
24/01	Jet Provost T3	XM360	CFS	Nr Abdon, Salop	Flew into ground
27/01	Harrier GR1	XV743	HSA	Nr Cranleigh, Surrey	Crashed during pre-delivery test flight; 1F (USMC pilot)
30/01	Hunter T8	XL585	769 Sqn	Portsay, Scotland	Crashed
31/01	Wessex HC2	XV727	A&AEE	Norway	Crashed in whiteout during cold weather trials
03/02	Hunter FGA9	XF508	20 Sqn	Off Johore, Malaysia	Abandoned over the sea; Ej
13/02	Buccaneer S2	XV346	736 Sqn	Dornoch Firth, Scotland	Crashed into sea
13/02	Meteor T7	WL350	FRADU	5nm SE Yeovilton	Flew into ground following roller landings at Yeovilton; 2F
03/03	Buccaneer S2	XN980	736 Sqn	10nm S of Wick	Abandoned over the sea following mid-air collision; Ej
03/03	Buccaneer S2	XV159	736 Sqn	10nm S of Wick	Abandoned over the sea following mid-air collision; Ej
03/03	Hunter GA11	XE680	738 Sqn	Rhayader, Wales	Crashed
18/03	Belvedere HC1	XG453	66 Sqn	–	Fire on start-up
25/03	Canberra PR9	XH130	13 Sqn	Nr Hal Far, Malta	Stalled on approach; 2F
26/03	Gnat T1	XR573	CFS	RAF Kemble	Hit trees attempting to regain formation during display practice (Red Arrows)
02/04	Hunter FGA9	XJ673	20 Sqn	Off Manila, Philippines	Abandoned over the sea; Ej
03/04	Sioux AH1	XT204	ARWS	Middle Wallop	Crashed following tail rotor failure
08/05	Alouette AH2	XR387	24 Flt	West Germany	Crashed on take-off due to cross-connection of control rods
13/05	Whirlwind HAR10	XP332	28 Sqn	Nr Brothers Is, HK	Crashed into sea following engine failure
14/05	Sioux AH1	XR640	6 Flt	Chattendon Barracks, Kent	Mid-air collision with Sioux XT802 during flying display

Date	Type	Serial	Unit	Location	Remarks
14/05	Sioux AH1	XT802	3 RTR	Chattendon Barracks, Kent	Mid-air collision with XT640
17/05	Wessex HU5	XT774	845 Sqn	HMS *Bulwark* off Dhekelia, Cyprus	Rolled on lift-off after dropping underslung load on carrier
21/05	Hunter FGA9	XE616	1 Sqn	Off Norfolk coast	Crashed into sea during low-level combat exercise; 1F
04/06	Harrier T2	XW174	HSA	Larkhill, Wilts	Crashed during delivery flight to Boscombe Down; Ej
06/06	Sea Vixen FAW2	XS584	893 Sqn	English Channel	Crashed into the sea off Hartland Point
07/06	Whirlwind HAR10	XP396	230 Sqn	Nr Leicester	Crashed following tail-rotor failure
13/06	Gnat T1	XP501	CFS	RAF Fairford	Undershot runway following hydraulic failure
13/06	Gnat T1	XR952	4FTS	Nr Conway, Wales	Abandoned in spin; Ej
20/06	Whirlwind HAS7	XL868	705 Sqn	Nr St Ives, Cornwall	Rolled over following force-landing on edge of disused mine shaft
09/07	Phantom FGR2	XV395	6 Sqn	Nr Horncastle, Lincs	First RAF Phantom loss
23/07	Chipmunk T10	WG488	4AEF	6nm E Woolacombe, Devon	Spun into ground
15/08	Hunter F6	XG204	4FTS	Nr Rhosneigr	Crashed after take-off
15/08	Sioux AH1	XT825	1 Wing	West Germany	Crashed into trees
21/08	Varsity T1	WJ895	5FTS	Nr Oakington	Landed safely following mid-air collision with a Cessna 150; DBR
25/08	Sioux AH1	XT509	Blue Eagles	Christchurch, Hants	Mid-air collision with Sioux XW191 during air display
25/08	Sioux AH1	XW191	Blue Eagles	Christchurch, Hants	Mid-air collision with XT509
02/09	Whirlwind HAS 7	XL881	771 Sqn	Nr Portland	Ditched in Channel following power loss
04/09	Jet Provost T3	XN576	CFS	Nr Northleach, Glos	Abandoned following engine failure; Ej
04/09	Sioux AH1	XR246	1RHA	Aden	Crashed following power failure
09/09	Wessex HAS1	XS126	820 Sqn	Irish Sea	Ditched in sea near HMS *Eagle*
16/09	Buccaneer S2	XV164	801 Sqn	5nm Strathy Point, Sunderland	Crashed into sea
22/09	Lightning F6	XS926	5 Sqn	North Sea	Abandoned over sea following loss of control; Ej
30/09	Jet Provost T3	XN575	3FTS	RAF Leeming	Stalled on take-off
23/10	Gannet AEW3	XP224	849 Sqn	HMS *Hermes*	Hit another Gannet on deck and fell into the sea
30/10	Whirlwind HAR10	XR477	28 Sqn	Nr Fanling, HK	Hit HT cables, lost rotor blades
31/10	Hunter T8	WW664	764 Sqn	Nr Lossiemouth	Crashed in sea

Date	Type	Serial	Unit	Location	Cause
17/11	Whirlwind HAR9	XM666	829 Sqn	Off Falklands	Ditched in sea near HMS *Endurance*
25/11	Wessex HAS3	XP153	826 Sqn	English Channel	Ditched in the sea near HMS *Eagle* following engine failure
26/11	Whirlwind HAR10	XP343	CFS	RAF Valley	Crashed following rotor striking tail boom
09/12	Wasp HAS1	XV637	829 Sqn	Off Portland	Fell into the sea off HMS *Londonderry*
16/12	Gnat T1	XR992	CFS	Nr Cirencester, Glos	Abandoned following report of engine fire (Red Arrows); Ej
16/12	Gnat T1	XR995	CFS	Nr Cirencester, Glos	Abandoned following erroneous report of engine fire (Red Arrows); Ej

1970

Date	Type	Serial	Unit	Location	Cause
03/01	Gnat T1	XR997	4FTS	Nr Llanfaelog, Wales	Crashed after take-off; 2F
29/01	Buccaneer S2	XV167	801 Sqn	HMS *Hermes*	Crashed on landing; DBR
11/02	Wessex HAS3	XP103	706 Sqn	Falmouth Bay	Ditched into sea following engine failure
27/02	Lightning F6	XS930	74 Sqn	Tengah, Singapore	Crashed on take-off
05/03	Lightning F6	XS918	11 Sqn	9nm E Leuchars	Abandoned following fire in flight; Ej
16/03	Jet Provost T4	XP576	3FTS	RAF Leeming	Abandoned on approach; Ej
17/03	Jet Provost T3	XN556	1FTS	RAF Linton-on-Ouse	Crashed on overshoot
19/03	Hunter FR10	XE596	229 OCU	Nr Paderborn, WG	Crashed following engine failure
22/04	Sioux HT2	XV310	CFS	Hinstock, Shropshire	Mid-air collision with Sioux XV316; 1F
22/04	Sioux HT2	XV316	CFS	Hinstock, Shropshire	Mid-air collision with XV310
30/04	Jet Provost T4	XP566	RAFC	RAF Cranwell	Crashed during night approach
01/05	Canberra TT18	WJ632	A&AEE	3nm SE Bridport	Crashed into the sea during target-towing trials
03/05	Phantom FG1	XV566	892 Sqn	Lyme Bay, Dorset	Crashed into sea; 2F
07/05	Lightning F3	XP742	111 Sqn	Nr Gt Yarmouth	Abandoned over sea following engine fire; Ej
16/05	Gannet AEW3	XR433	849 Sqn	RNAS Yeovilton	Crashed on night approach; 2F
26/05	Lightning F6	XR767	74 Sqn	50nm NW Singapore	Flew into sea at night; 1F
04/06	Argosy C1	XP441	114 Sqn	RAF Benson	Crashed on approach
11/06	Harrier GR1	XW264	HSA	Salisbury Plain	Flew into ground following loss of control

Date	Type	Serial	Unit	Location	Remarks
22/06	Jet Provost T3	XN469	1FTS	East Moor, Yorks	Crashed during emergency landing following engine failure
22/06	Whirlwind HAR10	XD183	103 Sqn	Nr Changi, Malaya	Force-landing following engine failure; DBR
26/06	Chipmunk T10	WZ861	Glasgow UAS	3nm SE Nairn, Scotland	Hit wall during force-landing
04/07	Harrier T2	XW264	A&AEE	Salisbury Plain	Abandoned following technical failure; Ej
13/07	Chipmunk T10	WK575	Wyton Flt	Laxfield, Sussex	Stalled during turn
27/07	Lightning F6	XS930	74 Sqn	Nr Tengah, Singapore	Spun into ground on take-off; 1F
27/07	Canberra B2	WH641	85 Sqn	RAF Wattisham	Spun into the ground on short finals; 3F
12/08	Wasp HAS1	XT789	929 Sqn	Mull of Kintyre	Ditched in sea off HMS *Dido*
12/08	Lightning F6	XS893	74 Sqn	18nm E Changi, Singapore	Abandoned following undercarriage jamming; Ej
26/08	Sea Vixen FAW2	XN686	A&AEE	Boscombe Down	Crashed on approach
31/08	Buccaneer S2	XT282	800 Sqn	Moray Firth	Abandoned over the sea following hydraulic failure; Ej
31/08	Sioux AH1	XT828	131 Flt	Korvach, WG	Crashed and burnt out
04/09	Sioux AH1	XT502	4/7 RDG	Aldergrove, NI	Crashed on landing
08/09	Lightning F6	XS894	5 Sqn	Nr Flamborough Head	Ditched; pilot never found
19/09	Lightning T4	XM990	226 OCU	Little Plumstead, Norfolk	Abandoned during low-level aerobatics at BofB Display following control failure; Ej
22/09	Hunter GA11	WT721	764 Sqn	Nr Blair Atholl	Crashed into hillside; 1F
06/10	Harrier GR1	XV796	1 Sqn	Ouston, Co Durham	Abandoned following flame-out; Ej
17/10	Whirlwind HAR10	XL109	28 Sqn	Hong Kong	Crashed
12/11	Wessex HC2	XR510	HOCF	RAF Odiham	Mid-air collision with XT679
12/11	Wessex HC2	XT679	HOCF	RAF Odiham	Mid-air collision with XR510
13/11	Gnat T1	XR994	CFS	RAF Kemble	Abandoned during practice formation aerobatics following engine failure (Red Arrows); Ej
13/11	Sea Vixen FAW2	XP955	899 Sqn	Moray Firth	Crashed into sea while operating from HMS *Eagle*
20/11	Whirlwind HAR10	XL112	202 Sqn	Patrick Brimpton, Yorks	Crashed on landing
08/12	Buccaneer S1	XN968	736 Sqn	SSW of Lossiemouth	Crashed into woods on approach
15/12	Canberra B(I)8	XM267	3 Sqn	RAF Akrotiri, Cyprus	Flew into ground on overshoot

Date	Type	Serial	Unit	Location	Cause
08/01	Vulcan B2	XM610	44 Sqn	Nr Wingate	Abandoned following engine fire; Ej
15/01	Wessex HU5	XS500	848 Sqn	Nr Porthleven	Flew into the sea in haze on approach to HMS *Bulwark*
18/01	Whirlwind HAR10	XJ432	28 Sqn	Sai Kung, HK	Force-landing following engine failure
20/01	Gnat T1	XR545	CFS	RAF Kemble	Mid-air collision during synchronised pair practice (Red Arrows); 2F
20/01	Gnat T1	XR986	CFS	RAF Kemble	Mid-air collision during synchronised pair practice (Red Arrows); 2F
24/01	Whirlwind HAR10	XP303	28 Sqn	Peak Alpha, HK	Hit obstacle and rolled over during hover; DBR
25/01	Lightning F3	XP756	29 Sqn	Nr Gt Yarmouth	Abandoned over sea following fire warning; Ej
28/01	Lightning F2	XN772	92 Sqn	Nr Diepholz, WG	Abandoned following loss of control during spin; Ej
29/01	Canberra T17	WH874	360 Sqn	Sutton-in-Ashfield, Notts	Mid-air collision with Canberra WJ862
29/01	Canberra T4	WJ862	360 Sqn	Sutton-in-Ashfield, Notts	Mid-air collision with WH874
24/02	Jet Provost T3	XN465	3FTS	Nr Easingwold, Yorks	Spun into ground; Ej
02/03	Jet Provost T5	XW300	1FTS	Nr Church Fenton	Mid-air collision with Sea Prince WP312
02/03	Sea Prince T1	WP312	RN Flt	Nr Church Fenton	Mid-air collision with XW300
19/03	Hunter F6	XG131	229 OCU	Exmoor	Flew into high ground
25/03	Buccaneer S2	XW532	12 Sqn	Nr Laarbruch, WG	Crashed during low-level flight
23/04	Harrier GR1	XV798	20 Sqn	RAF Wildenrath, WG	Loss of control on approach to vertical landing; Ej
28/04	Lightning F6	XS938	23 Sqn	12nm E Leuchars	Abandoned following fuel fire during take-off; Ej
10/05	Lightning F3	XP744	29 Sqn	15nm W Akrotiri, Cyprus	Abandoned over sea following fire warning; Ej
14/05	Beaver AL1	XP807	132 Flt	Nr Batteln, WG	Crashed during a thunderstorm; 1F
17/05	Hunter T7	XL622	4FTS	Nr Blaenau Ffestiniog	Flew into high ground
19/05	Phantom FG1	XT862	767 Sqn	25nm NW Newquay, Cornwall	Abandoned over sea; Ej
20/05	Wessex HAS1	XM875	771 Sqn	Off Portland	Crashed into the sea
20/05	Lightning F3	XP752	111 Sqn	Nr Colmar, France	Mid-air collision with Mirage IIIE; DBR
26/05	Lightning F6	XS902	5 Sqn	15nm NE Grimsby	Abandoned over sea following engine fires; Ej
05/06	Buccaneer S2A	XN978	12 Sqn	28nm NE Le Bourget, France	Lost control while air-to-air refuelling at low-level; Ej

Vulcan Crashes

Ever since the notorious crash of one of Britain's new breed of V-bombers at Heathrow airport in September 1956 on the last leg of a triumphant tour to Australia — the type's first overseas flight — it was clear that those members of Vulcan crews not having the benefit of ejector seats were extremely vulnerable in the event of low-level emergencies. The only surviving members of the six-man crew involved in the Heathrow accident were the pilot and co-pilot, the latter being AM Sir Harry Broadhurst, who ejected at extremely low-level.

However, on 8 January 1971, all the crew of Vulcan B2 XM610 of No 44 Squadron were able to abandon their aircraft successfully and without injury following an in-flight emergency. Following a loud explosion from the rear port side of the Vulcan, fire broke out in the engine compartment while the aircraft was flying at 15,000ft over the Cheviot Hills on a routine training flight from its base at RAF Waddington. After losing height to 9,000ft over Rothbury in Northumberland, the captain, 27-year-old Flt Lt Garth Alcock, ordered the two navigators and the electronics officer to bale out of their 'downstairs' office through the only exit in an emergency — a protected hatch in the floor of the fuselage. All landed safely while Garth Alcock and his co-pilot attempted to fly the crippled bomber to RAF Leeming in Yorkshire with a view to making an emergency landing. This proved to be impossible as the fire had gained such a hold in and around the engine bay that there was a very real possiblity of the aircraft exploding in mid-air.

After heading the Vulcan out to sea over Whitley Bay, the co-pilot ejected, having already blown the canopy, followed a few minutes later by

Flt Lt Alcock. Both landed without injury.

However, as soon as it was abandoned, XM160 began a gentle descending turn to starboard and continued flying steadily for another 80 miles during which time it circled Sunderland before eventually crashing on waste ground on the outskirts of Wingate in County Durham. Although many of Wingate's inhabitants had witnessed the explosion as the Vulcan hit the ground, there was no damage to property and, more important, no-one was injured by the flaming debris. If the aircraft had remained airborne for just another minute, it might well have been a different story.

Four years later, another Vulcan also crashed on the outskirts of a small village, but this time with tragic results. Vulcan B2, XM645, belonging to No 9 Squadron left its base at RAF Waddington early on 14 October 1975 with a crew of seven for a routine training flight to RAF Luqa in Malta. After an uneventful transit flight, XM645 began a normal let-down to Luqa in clear weather and excellent visibility. For some reason, the Vulcan made a heavy landing and the captain made the decision to overshoot. However, during his climb-out, he was informed by Luqa's Air Traffic Control that 'your undercarriage is on the runway'. When the aircraft had touched down, the Vulcan's port undercarriage leg had been ripped off and a wing and tailcone damaged. Although the aircraft had managed to take-off and climb into a circuit in preparation for an emergency

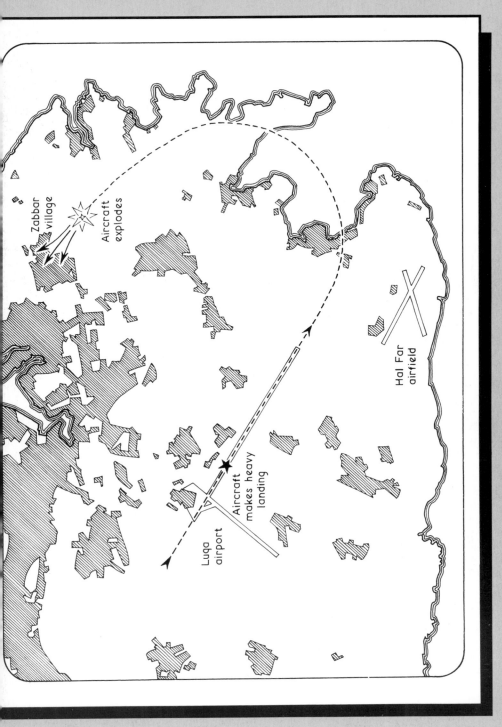

Zabbar village

Aircraft explodes

Hal Far airfield

Aircraft makes heavy landing

Luqa airport

landing, it was obviously seriously damaged. Witnesses reported seeing flames coming from the wings shortly before the Vulcan exploded in mid-air over Zabbar village some four miles northeast of Luqa. The pilot and co-pilot managed to eject safely but the aircraft was too low for the remaining members of the crew to bale out. Sqn Ldr I. D. W. Beeden, Flt Lts G. A. Pulman and E. S. Lamber, Chief Tech T. J. Barrow and Sgt P. J. Atkins, were all killed in the crash. A 20-year-old woman was also killed on the ground and 20 people injured as blazing debris from the aircraft fell on the village of 9,000 people, demolishing 12 houses and several cars, one of which belonged to a British honeymoon couple who narrowly escaped injury.

The bulk of the wreckage fell on waste ground on the outskirts of the village close to a school. Royal Navy helicopters from HMS *Hermes* in Valletta Harbour were sent to the scene of the crash immediately to assist local emergency services.

There were other Vulcan accidents that highlighted the shortsighted policy of not equipping all crew-members with ejector seats: a No 101 Squadron Vulcan crashed near Spilsby, Lincs, in January 1977 following an engine fire, and a No 617 Squadron B2 struck the ground soon after take-off during an air display at Glenview NAS in the United States. In both these accidents, some crew members survived thanks to their ejector seats.

This was a classic example of cost-cutting versus flight safety which meant that Vulcan crews, apart from the pilot and co-pilot who were equipped with ejector seats, had a very slim chance of successfully abandoning a stricken aircraft at low-level.

Below:
Vulcan B2 XM645 about to touch down at RAF Luqa, Malta, on 14 October 1975.

Date	Type	Serial	Unit	Location	Remarks
29/06	Phantom FG1	XV565	892 Sqn	Off Florida Coast, USA	Crashed into sea; Ej
29/06	Jet Provost T3	XN558	3FTS	RAF Dishforth	Abandoned following bird ingestion on approach; Ej
06/07	Sea Vixen FAW2	XN687	890 Sqn	Charlton Horethorne, Somerset	Crashed after take-off from Yeovilton
08/07	Lightning F3	XP705	29 Sqn	35nm S Akrotiri, Cyprus	Abandoned over sea following engine failure; Ej
14/07	Wessex HAS3	XP147	737 Sqn	Off Portland	Ditched in the sea
03/08	Harrier GR1	XV803	1 Sqn	Nr Wattisham	Crashed on landing following nozzle valve failure; 1F (USAF pilot)
22/08	Whirlwind HAR10	XJ426	22 Sqn	Nr Lundy Is	Ditched in sea during CASEVAC following fire warning
03/08	Harrier GR1	XV803	1 Sqn	Nr Peterborough, Cambs	Abandoned after take-off from Wittering; Ej; 1F (Capt L. Distelzweig USAF)
27/08	Hunter F6	XG229	229 OCU	Merton, Devon	Abandoned following flying controls seizure; Ej
22/09	Lightning F3	XP736	29 Sqn	40nm NE Gt Yarmouth	Dived into sea; 1F
30/09	Lightning F6	XR764	56 Sqn	35nm E Akrotiri, Cyprus	Abandoned over sea following engine fire; Ej
05/10	Canberra B(I)8	WT366	16 Sqn	Luttingen, Holland	Flew into ground after take-off
06/10	Canberra B15	WH973	98 Sqn	3nm S Cottesmore	Abandoned following loss of control on approach; Ej
09/10	Hunter FGA9	XG156	229 OCU	Gibraltar	Crashed on landing following u/c failure; Ej; 1F
12/10	Phantom FGR2	XV479	54 Sqn	Nr Karup, Denmark	Abandoned following engine failure; Ej
15/10	Phantom FGR2	XT904	228 OCU	Nr Coningsby	Abandoned over sea off Cromer following loss of control during spin; Ej
29/10	Lightning F3	XR711	111 Sqn	RAF Wattisham	Stalled on take-off following premature rotation; 1F
08/11	Hunter T7	XL575	4 FTS	Nr Devil's Bridge, Dyfed	Flew into ground
09/11	Hercules C1	XV216	–	17nm E Pisa, Italy	Crashed into sea
15/11	Wessex HAS3	XP116	737 Sqn	Off Portland	Crashed into the sea
09/12	Buccaneer S2	XV347	12 Sqn	RAF Lossiemouth	Fire on runway, DBR
13/12	Gnat T1	XR567	CFS	Nr Upper Heyford	Crashed on approach

1972

Date	Type	Serial	Unit	Location	Cause
04/01	Buccaneer S2	XW539	12 Sqn	Irish Sea	Flew into sea
06/01	Wessex HAS3	XP104	820 Sqn	Mediterranean	Ditched in sea off Malta
10/01	Phantom FG1	XT876	767 Sqn	Trevose Head, Cornwall	Abandoned over the sea; Ej
12/01	Harrier GR1	XW918	3 Sqn	Nr Wildenrath, WG	Failed to recover from dive during demonstration; 1F
13/01	Sea King HAS1	XV645	737 Sqn	Off Portland	Ditched in sea
19/01	Gnat T1	XR996	CFS	Nr Pershore	Abandoned following compressor failure; Ej
20/01	Wasp HAS1	XV628	829 Sqn	Malaysia	Crashed into coconut plantation
04/02	Sioux AH1	XT106	3CBAS	Woodhouse Eaves, Leics	Crashed
09/02	Chipmunk T10	WB552	AEF	Nr Bicester	Lost control during spin; 2F
14/02	Phantom FGR2	XT913	228 OCU	North Sea	Abandoned over sea following hydraulic failure; Ej
15/02	Buccaneer S2	XT269	809 Sqn	HMS *Ark Royal*	Rolled off the side and sank in the Atlantic
16/02	Wessex HAS3	XS121	737 Sqn	Off Portland	Ditched in the sea
16/02	Lightning F3	XP698	29 Sqn	60nm E Harwich	Mid-air collision over sea with XP747; Ej
16/02	Lightning F3	XP747	29 Sqn	60nm E Harwich	Mid-air collision over sea
14/03	Gnat T1	XR948	4FTS	Nr Llanbedr, Wales	Abandoned following engine failure; Ej
21/03	Harrier GR1	XV802	20 Sqn	Nr Hanover, WG	Flew into ground
08/04	Andover C1	XS609	46 Sqn	Nr Sienna, Italy	Wing hit ground during take-off following engine failure
26/04	Harrier GR1	XV749	1 Sqn	Theddlethorpe	Abandoned following birdstrike; Ej
01/05	Harrier GR1	XV777	1 Sqn	RAF Wittering	Abandoned following loss of control; Ej
04/05	Harrier GR1	XV794	4 Sqn	RAF Wildenrath	Abandoned following birdstrike and flew on for 40min before running out of fuel; Ej
13/06	Buccaneer S2	XV162	12 Sqn	Nr Bridlington	Flew into sea in bad visibility; 2F
20/06	Harrier GR1A	XW920	3 Sqn	Deccimomannu, Sardinia	Abandoned following fuel unit failure; Ej
26/06	Canberra B2	WJ610	85 Sqn	Nr West Raynham	Crashed following loss of control in cloud; F
26/06	Sea Heron C1	XR444	781 Sqn	Irish Sea	Ditched in sea following loss of power on all four engines
27/06	Harrier GR1A	XV780	4 Sqn	Nr Wildenrath, WG	Abandoned following birdstrike; Ej

Date	Type	Serial	Unit	Location	Cause
29/06	Gannet AEW3	XL474	849 Sqn	RNAS Yeovilton	Crashed on approach
07/07	Sioux AH1	XT114	663 Sqn	Otterburn	Crashed and burnt out during Operation 'Skywarrior'
07/08	Lightning F3	XP700	29 Sqn	Nr Wattisham	Struck runway after take-off
10/08	Hunter F6	XF387	4FTS	Nr Valley	Mid-air collision with XF384; Ej
10/08	Hunter F6	XF384	4FTS	Nr Valley	Mid-air collision with Hunter XF387; Ej
28/08	Wessex HU5	XT454	845 Sqn	Liskeard, Cornwall	Crashed after hitting power lines
30/08	Hiller HT2	XS161	705 Sqn	Goonhilly Downs	Crashed landed and broke-up
06/09	Lightning T5	XS455	5 Sqn	Nr Spurn Head	Abandoned following hydraulic failure; Ej
12/09	Harrier GR1	XV799	233 OCU	Scotland	Flew into ground; 1F
12/09	Jet Provost T5A	XW356	RAFC	Nr Cranwell	Crashed following loss of control in cloud; 1F
27/09	Puma HC1	XW218	230 Sqn	Nr Thetford, Norfolk	Tail rotor struck ground; DBR
27/09	Wessex HU5	XS490	845 Sqn	Norway	Crashed in whiteout
06/10	Buccaneer S2	XV339	Shorts	Castlereagh, NI	Crashed on test flight
06/10	Canberra PR9	XH172	13 Sqn	Akrotiri, Cyprus	Crashed following loss of control
01/11	Hunter GA11	WV381	ADS	RNAS Lee-on-Solent	Ran into sea following unsuccessful take-off due to power loss
21/11	Whirlwind HAR9	XL900	SAR Flt	RNAS Culdrose	Lost tail rotor and broke up
21/11	Phantom FGR2	XV477	6 Sqn	9nm E Penrith	Flew into high ground
22/11	Lynx HAS2	XX469	Westland	Yeovil	Crashed on airfield following loss of tail rotor control (First Lynx accident)
13/12	Whirlwind HAR10	XP349	22 Sqn	Holyhead Harbour	Ditched in sea following engine failure
14/12	Lightning T4	XM974	226 OCU	Nr Happisburgh, Northumbs	Abandoned following engine failure; Ej

1973

Date	Type	Serial	Unit	Location	Cause
24/01	Buccaneer S2	XW535	16 Sqn	Nr Lübeck, WG	Crashed following loss of control
06/02	Whirlwind HAR10	XL110	84 Sqn	RAF Nicosia, Cyprus	Main rotor detached during ground run
06/02	Sioux AH1	XT127	3CBAS	Camp Lejeune, N Carolina USA	Crashed into the New River estuary during an exercise with the USMC

Date	Type	Serial	Unit	Location	Details
07/02	Puma HC1	XW214	33 Sqn	Aldergrove, NI	Rotor blades struck hangar; DBR
27/02	Sioux AH1	XT836	661 Sqn	Detmold, WG	Crashed on take-off during whiteout
11/03	Jet Provost T5	XW331	3FTS	RAF Leeming	Heavy landing; DBR
27/03	Hunter FGA9	XG256	229 OCU	Nr Liskeard, Cornwall	Abandoned following wirestrike; Ej
03/04	Lightning F6	XS934	56 Sqn	Nr Akrotiri, Cyprus	Abandoned following engine fire; Ej
06/04	Hunter FGA9	XG135	45 Sqn	Nr Wittering	Abandoned following fire warning; Ej
12/04	Buccaneer S2	XV343	809 Sqn	Nr Honington	Crashed on approach
16/04	Whirlwind HAR9	XN310	Lee-on-Solent SAR Flt	English Channel	Ditched and sank off South Coast
18/04	Sioux AH1	XT174	666 Sqn	Caledon, Co Tyrone, NI	Crashed after hitting power line
23/04	Vulcan B2	XJ781	9 Sqn	Shiraz, Iran	U/c collapsed on landing; DBR
05/05	Sioux AH1	XT503	3CBAS	Mediterranean	Ditched in sea off Crete while operating from HMS *Bulwark*
07/05	Jet Provost T4	XR647	6FTS	Norton-le-Clay, Yorks	Mid-air collision with XS216; Ej
10/05	Victor SR2	XL230	543 Sqn	RAF Wyton	Crashed during night overshoot due to loss of control; 5F
01/06	Phantom FGR2	XV397	17 Sqn	WG	Abandoned following instrument failure; Ej
05/06	Hunter FGA9	XG169	229 OCU	Nr Holsworthy	Abandoned following engine failure; Ej
05/06	Lightning T4	XM988	226 OCU	Nr Gt Yarmouth	Abandoned over sea following loss of control during spin; Ej
05/06	Lightning F3	XR719	56 Sqn	RAF Coltishall	Heavy landing; DBR
12/06	Gannet AEW3	XP229	849 Sqn	English Channel	Ditched in sea while operating from HMS *Ark Royal*
25/06	Phantom FGR2	XV440	31 Sqn	Nr Vlieboss, Holland	Flew into sea at night; 2F
28/06	Harrier GR3	XW919	1 Sqn	RAF Lyneham	Abandoned following loss of power; Ej
07/07	Sioux AH1	XT238	16/15 QRL	Aldridge, Staffs	Crashed following loss of control during attempted rescue of parachutist hanging from HT wires
05/07	Basset CC1	XS783	26 Sqn	Nr Valley	Force-landing following loss of power due to incorrect fuel; DBR
09/07	Harrier GR3	XV791	20 Sqn	RAF Wildenrath, WG	Abandoned following birdstrike; Ej
25/07	Phantom FG1	XT871	892 Sqn	Firth of Forth	Crashed into sea
27/07	Hunter F6	XF420	229 OCU	Chawleigh, Devon	Abandoned following engine failure; Ej
28/07	Gnat T1	XR993	4FTS	RNAS Lee-on-Solent	Emergency landing following birdstrike and engine damage; DBR
30/07	Harrier GR1A	XV805	20 Sqn	Nr Coesfeld, WG	Abandoned following birdstrike; Ej (USMC pilot)

Date	Type	Serial	Unit	Location	Cause
02/08	Canberra B2	WJ674	231 OCU	RAF Cottesmore	Lost control during overshoot
07/08	Gazelle AH1	XW850	1FTU	Fordingbridge	Crashed following jack-stall during intensive trials (First AAC Gazelle accident)
22/08	Phantom FGR2	XV427	17 Sqn	WG	Flew into high ground
06/09	Gnat T1	XP508	4FTS	Nr Valley	Abandoned following loss of power; Ej
06/09	Harrier GR3	XV750	20 Sqn	Nr Wildenrath, WG	Abandoned following engine failure; Ej
10/09	Hercules C1	XV198	LTW	RAF Colerne	Stalled on roller take-off following engine run-down; 5F
16/09	Sioux AH1	XT185	3CBAS	Mediterranean	Ditched in sea off Malta
24/09	Harrier GR1A	XV739	1 Sqn	Cyprus	Crashed following loss of control; Ej
12/10	Gnat T1	XR537	4FTS	Nr Leeming	Force-landing following birdstrike
15/10	Phantom FG1	XT869	892 Sqn	Tentsmuir Forest, Scotland	Crashed on approach to Leuchars
02/11	Hunter T7	XL596	4FTS	Nr Shawbury	Crashed into trees on approach
06/11	Sea Vixen FAW2	XP954	FRADU	Ashington, Somerset	Crashed following engine failure
27/11	Varsity T1	WF411	CFS	RAF Little Rissington	Lost control on aborted roller take-off; DBR
10/12	Lightning F3	XP738	111 Sqn	RAF Wattisham	U/c failure on landing; DBR
12/12	Wasp HAS1	XT442	BRNC	Norton heliport, Dartmouth	Crashed on take-off

1974

Date	Type	Serial	Unit	Location	Cause
23/01	Harrier GR3	XV797	4 Sqn	Vreedepeel, Holland	Loss of control following flap drive assembly failure; Ej; 1F
13/02	Lightning F3	XR715	29 Sqn	Blyford Green, Southwold	Abandoned following engine fires; Ej
14/02	Hunter F6	XG161	229 OCU	Nr Chivenor	Crashed into sea during formation flight; 1F
18/02	Wessex HU5	XT477	845 Sqn	Nr Harstad, Norway	Crashed into sea
21/03	Sea King HAS1	XV702	824 Sqn	Nr Lizard	Crashed into cliff
26/03	Harrier GR3	XV785	4 Sqn	RAF Wildenrath, WG	Crashed after landing following loss of control
12/04	Scout AH1	XR636	664 Sqn	Armagh, NI	Hit rising ground during low-level flight
16/05	Harrier GR3	XV800	4 Sqn	RAF Wildenrath, WG	Abandoned following birdstrike; Ej

9 Aug 1974: Pawnee G-ASVK and Phantom FGR2 XV493

On the afternoon of 9 August 1974, Piper PA25 Pawnee crop-spraying aircraft, G-ASVK, chartered from ADS Aerial of Southend, was returning to its local operations centre having completed its task of spraying potato fields at Denver Sluice near Downham Market in Norfolk. Minutes later an RAF Phantom collided with the Pawnee and the two aircraft plunged into a wheatfield. The Phantom's two-man crew and the Pawnee's pilot, 24-year-old New Zealander Paul Hickmott were killed outright in the crash. The collision occurred in good visibility at an estimated height of 300ft.

The Phantom FGR2, XV493, belonging to No 41 Squadron from RAF Coningsby in Lincolnshire, had taken off from its base for a routine low-level navigation and reconnaissance exercise. The pilot was 42-year-old Gp Capt David Blucke, Coningsby's Station Commander. His navigator was 28-year-old Flt Lt Terence Kirkland.

The crew had requested permission to fly at low level via the Holbeach Range, situated on the southern edge of The Wash, to Norfolk which would take it over Downham Market some 40 miles southeast of Coningsby, an area frequently used for low-level flying by the RAF. The authorisation limited the aircraft's height to not less than 250 AGL with a speed of 420kt to be maintained.

Civilian authorities had been advised of the Pawnee's intention to work in the area and as it was going to be flying on a recognised low-level route frequented by military traffic, the closest airfield, RAF Marham, had been informed that aerial spraying would be carried out in the area from June to August. There was no requirement, however, to notify each other of specific flights at specific times.

As a result of the collision, in which the navigator was ejected through the canopy, wreckage was scattered over a wide area and although RAF SAR helicopters were sent to the scene from

Coningsby and Coltishall, it was immediately apparent that nobody could have survived the accident.

Although only two civilians had died on the ground as a direct result of military mid-air collisions in the UK since 1945, this particular accident prompted numerous protests from residents living in the Downham Market area and demands from local MPs that low-level flying by the RAF should be banned in the area. Due to the unusually high amount of public interest there were strong demands for the reports of the inquiries into the accident, which were being carried out by both the MoD and Department of Trade, should be made public. In the event it was almost a year before W. H. Tench, the Chief Inspector of Accidents of the AIB, published his report for the Department of Trade.

The official cause of the accident was that neither pilot saw the other aircraft in time to avoid collision. The 'see and be seen' was inadequate for preventing collision in the circumstances that existed. A significant feature which contributed to the accident was given as the absence of any system for co-ordinating military and civil low flying activities in the low-flying areas and link routes.

Although the Report went on to recommend that civil aircraft frequently engaged in low-level flying within known military low-flying areas should be painted as conspicuously as possible and that both civil and military types should be fitted with strobe collision warning lights, its main recommendation was for wider publication of military low-flying routes in the UK. It was considered essential that closer liaison between the military and civil aviation authorities should be achieved if this sort of unfortunate accident was to be avoided in the future.

Phantom FGR2 XV493 of No 41 Squadron collided with Pawnee G-ASVX at Denver Sluice near Downham Market on 9 August 1974.
A. Hancock via A. Goodrum

Date	Type	Serial	Unit	Location	Cause
07/06	Hunter FGA9	XG130	45 Sqn	Melton Mowbray	Crashed following loss of control
19/06	Scout AH1	XR631	664 Sqn	WG	Crashed following wirestrike
24/06	Lightning F3	XR748	29 Sqn	Nr Coltishall	Abandoned over sea following double hydraulic failure; Ej
15/07	Wessex HAS3	XP138	737 Sqn	Off Chesil Beach	Flew into sea during night training flight; 3F
09/08	Phantom FGR2	XV493	41 Sqn	Nr Bexwell, Norfolk	Mid-air collision with Pawnee crop-spraying aircraft at low-level; 3F
03/09	Hiller HT2	XS162	705 Sqn	Nr Culdrose	Crashed in field
09/09	Jaguar T2	XX144	OCU	RAF Lossiemouth	Bellylanding due to u/c failure: DBR
11/10	Phantom FGR2	XV431	31 Sqn	RAF Brüggen, WG	Abandoned following take-off with wings unlocked; Ej
20/10	Harrier GR3	XV758	3 Sqn	RAF Wildenrath, WG	Abandoned following loss of power on take-off; Ej
23/10	Sioux AH1	XT163	FARELF	Malaysia	Hit trees following disorientation during night flight
29/10	Lightning F6	XR768	5 Sqn	13nm E Saltfleet, Lincs	Abandoned following double reheat fire; Ej
01/11	Jetstream T1	XX477	CFS	RAF Little Rissington	Crashed following double engine failure on roller landing
11/11	Buccaneer S2	XV351	809 Sqn	The Wash	Crashed into the sea
15/11	Puma HC1	XW203	33 Sqn	Nr North Whitchurch	Crashed following loss of control; DBR
19/11	Sea King HAS1	XV644	737 Sqn	Off Portland	Ditched in sea and sank following flotation bags failure
21/11	Phantom FGR2	XV441	21 Sqn	Nr Brüggen, WG	Crashed following engine fire on take-off; Ej
22/11	Jaguar T2	XX136	A&AEE	Wimborne St Giles, Dorset	Crashed following engine fire
12/12	Sea King HAS1	XV667	826 Sqn	Bay of Biscay	Ditched in sea off HMS *Tiger*
16/12	Harrier GR3	XV779	3 Sqn	RAF Wildenrath, WG	Bellylanding following hydraulic failure

1975

Date	Type	Serial	Unit	Location	Cause
27/01	Whirlwind HAS9	XN311	Lee-on-Solent SAR Flt	Peel Common	Crashed on landing
13/02	Gazelle AH1	XW901	WHL	Suffield Range, Alberta, Canada	Crashed into lake during cold weather trails

Date	Type	Serial	Unit	Location	Remarks
03/03	Phantom FGR2	XV416	111 Sqn	River Witham	Abandoned following engine failure; Ej
17/03	Sioux AH1	XT225	ARWS	Middle Wallop	Heavy landing during downwind training
24/03	Victor K1A	XH618	57 Sqn	Nr Sunderland	Mid-air collision with Buccaneer XV156 over sea; 4F
28/03	Sioux AH1	XT840	3RTR	Belize	Overpitch during landing
09/04	Harrier GR3	XV776	1 Sqn	RAF Wittering	Abandoned following engine flame-out; Ej
14/04	Lightning F6	XR762	11 Sqn	Nr Akrotiri, Cyprus	Crashed into sea during tail chase; 1F
15/04	Sioux AH1	XT242	Blue Eagles	Middle Wallop	Main rotor hit ground during display training
30/04	Jaguar T2	XX831	226 OCU	RAF Lossiemouth	Loss of control from fouled control column during low inverted run
08/05	Wessex HAS1	XS880	Ark Royal SAR Flt	Off Salvador, Brazil	Ditched in the sea off HMS Ark Royal
22/05	Puma HC1	XW212	33 Sqn	Aldergrove, NI	Gearbox cowling became detached; DBR
30/05	Sioux AH1	XT547	657 Sqn	Soltau, WG	Heavy landing following overpitch during take-off; DBR
04/06	Wasp HAS1	XT424	829 Sqn	English Channel	Crashed into sea while operating from HMS Juno
16/06	Sioux AH1	XT164	664 Sqn	Farnborough	Heavy landing following main rotor tie rod failure; DBR
16/07	Buccaneer S2B	XW536	15 Sqn	North Sea, off Denmark	Abandoned following mid-air collision with Buccaneer XW528; Ej
29/07	Buccaneer S2A	XV360	237 OCU	North Sea off Southwold	Flew into sea following loss of control
29/07	Chipmunk T10	WB562	7AEF	Nr Winthorpe	Crashed following loss of control; 1F
21/08	Wessex HAS3	XM871	737 Sqn	Indian Ocean	Crashed into sea following take-off from HMS Glamorgan with deck tether attached
03/09	Gnat T1	XS103	CFS	Nr Leck, WG	Mid-air collision with Italian AF F104S; DBR
11/09	Bulldog T1	XX557	Glasgow UAS	Nr Glasgow	Hit trees on low-level flight
17/09	Wessex HAS1	XP112	Ark Royal SAR Flt	English Channel	Ditched in the sea off HMS Ark Royal
18/09	Phantom FG1	XV580	43 Sqn	2nm S of Kirriemuir, Scotland	Abandoned during rehearsal of formation 'Canadian Break'; Ej
25/09	Whirlwind HAR10	XP327	225 Sqn	45nm from Kuching, Malaysia	Crashed in jungle following engine failure and main rotor cutting through fuselage
30/09	Sioux AH1	XT849	AAC	WG	Heavy landing following overpitch during emergency wire avoidance; DBR

Date	Type	Serial	Unit	Location	Cause
14/10	Vulcan B2	XM645	9 Sqn	Zabbar, Malta	Broke-up in flight following heavy landing in undershoot at Luqa; 6F
16/10	Gnat T1	XS106	4FTS	Nr Llanwrst, Wales	Abandoned following loss of control in spin; Ej
17/11	Sea King HAS1	XV695	819 Sqn	North Sea	Lost off HMS *Hermes* during exercise
24/11	Phantom FGR2	XV405	228 OCU	Nr Coningsby	Abandoned following loss of control; Ej
01/12	Sioux AH1	XT113	666 Sqn	Belize	Crashed after running out of fuel
01/12	Harrier GR3	XV788	1 Sqn	Belize	Abandoned following engine problems; Ej
17/12	Phantom FGR2	XV463	41 Sqn	Nr Mawbury, Scotland	Flew into Solway Firth following loss of control; 2F
18/12	Sioux AH1	XW195	659 Sqn	Crossmaglen, NI	Crashed following wirestrike
18/12	Sioux AH1	XT818	662 Sqn	NI	Flew into power lines in fog

1976

Date	Type	Serial	Unit	Location	Cause
07/01	Scout AH1	XV133	662 Sqn	Armagh, NI	Aircraft hit high ground following nitesun disorientation
16/01	Wessex HU5	XT758	848 Sqn	English Channel	Ditched in the sea off HMS *Bulwark*
19/01	Harrier GR3	XV745	235 OCU	Nr Crewe	Mid-air collision with Harrier XV754; 1F
19/01	Harrier GR3	XV754	1 Sqn	Nr Crewe	Mid-air collision with Harrier XV745; 1F
22/01	Hunter T7A	XL579	ETPS	Winterbourne Gunner, Wilts	Crashed on approach
05/02	Jaguar T2	XX137	226 OCU	Nr Milltown	Abandoned over sea following double flame-out; Ej
13/02	Jet Provost T4	XS211	SRF	RAF Leeming	Abandoned following undershot landing following fuel starvation; Ej
03/03	Buccaneer S2B	XV166	15 Sqn	Nr Honington	Crashed on approach following loss of control in stall
12/03	Harrier GR3	XV746	233 OCU	Norway	Crashed into mountain
18/03	Vulcan B2	XL384	617 Sqn	RAF Scampton	–
19/03	Wessex HC2	XS678	ETPS	Salisbury Plain	Heavy landing; DBR
21/04	Hunter F6	XG185	4FTS	Maltreath Sands, Wales	Abandoned over sea following engine fire; Ej
27/04	Argosy C1	XR105	ETPS	Boscombe Down	Hit building following wing drop on asymmetric approach; 2F

Victor K2 XL513. *David Oliver*

30/04	Gnat T1	XP536	4FTS	Nr Dolgellau	Mid-air collision with Gnat at low-level; 2F
30/04	Gnat T1	XR983	4FTS	Nr Dolgellau	Mid-air collision with Gnat at low-level; 2F
04/05	Hunter FGA9	XJ635	TWU	Nr Aberystwyth	Crashed following loss of control; 1F
25/05	Gazelle AH1	XW900	660 Sqn	WG	Crashed following NVG disorientation
03/06	Bulldog T1	XX703	Edinburgh UAS	Glenrothes airfield, Fife	Force-landing following engine failure; DBR
13/06	Whirlwind HAR10	XP357	202 Sqn	Newgate Beach, nr Brawdy	Force-landing; DBR
24/06	Gnat T1	XS111	CFS	RAF Kemble	Undercarriage raised on landing following brake failure; DBR
02/07	Jaguar GR1	XX822	14 Sqn	Nr Cloppenburg, WG	Flew into ground during armaments practice; 1F
06/07	Harrier GR3	XW770	3 Sqn	Nr Borken, WG	Abandoned following engine failure; Ej
22/07	Bulldog T1	XX618	Yorkshire UAS	Nr Southport	Crashed following loss of control during spin

45

Date	Type	Serial	Unit	Location	Cause
23/07	Phantom FGR2	XV417	29 Sqn	Nr Mablethorpe	Abandoned following structural failure of starboard wing; Ej
30/07	Lightning F6	XS937	11 Sqn	Nr Spurn Head	Abandoned following u/c failure; Ej
03/08	Sioux AH1	XT115	–	Belize	Rolled off HLS
16/08	Hunter F6	XG191	1TWU	30nm SW of Brawdy	Crashed into sea
26/08	Wasp HAS1	XS544	829 Sqn	Nr Forth Bridge	Crashed into sea during flying display for crew and families of HMS *Yarmouth*
27/08	Puma HC1	XW230	1563Flt	Toledo, Belize	Force-landing following engine failure; DBR
15/09	Jaguar GR1	XX735	6 Sqn	Eggebeck, WG	Crashed following loss of control; 1F
17/09	Jaguar GR1	XX120	54 Sqn	Nr Samsoe Is, Denmark	Flew into sea; 1F
21/09	Hunter T8	WT772	FRADU	Nr Yeovil	Crashed on take-off from Yeovilton following engine failure
28/09	Victor K2	XL513	55 Sqn	RAF Marham	Crashed on overshoot following birdstrike on take-off; DBR
08/10	Gnat T1	XR996	4FTS	RAF Shawbury	Crashed on approach
11/10	Wessex HAS1	XS884	771 Sqn	Cornwall	Ditched in sea
25/10	Hunter FGA9	XJ636	1TWU	Mathry, Wales	Crashed on take-off from Brawdy following engine failure
29/10	Buccaneer S2B	XW531	12 Sqn	Bodo, Norway	Crashed following loss of control
13/12	Wessex HAS3	XM844	737 Sqn	Off the Scilly Isles	Crashed into the sea on take-off from HMS *Devonshire*
14/12	Jaguar GR1	XZ102	2 Sqn	Nr Laarbruch, WG	Loss of control following disconnected aileron

1977

Date	Type	Serial	Unit	Location	Cause
02/01	Sioux AH1	XT241	3 Flt	NI	Crashed into river following wirestrike
04/01	Gazelle AH1	XX461	GCF	Middle Wallop	Struck ground during hover
17/01	Vulcan B2	XM600	101 Sqn	Nr Spilsby, Lincs	Crashed following engine fire
03/02	Buccaneer S2B	XW548	16 Sqn	Nr Vokel, WG	Abandoned following engine fire at low-level; Ej
24/02	Lightning T4	XM968	92 Sqn	Nr Gutersloh, WG	Abandoned following hydraulic failure; Ej

13 June 1977: RN Sharks Aerobatic Team

At the end of 1974 the Royal Navy decided to form a helicopter formation team comprising six Gazelle HT2s flown by volunteer instructors drawn from 705 Sqn, the RN Helicopter School at RNAS Culdrose, Cornwall. The new team, christened the 'Sharks', was set to carry on the tradition of 'Fred's Five', a Sea Vixen team of the 1960s, and the 'Blue Herons' — six FRADU Hunters that made a brief appearance at the end of the 1970s. The Sharks were the only helicopter formation team to use six aircraft.

After two successful seasons, during which the Sharks built up a well-deserved reputation for their entertaining close-formation routines and thoroughly professional display — flying only a quarter of a rotor diameter apart — well into the 1977 season, it was preparing for an appearance at the Queen's Jubilee Review of the Fleet at Spithead in June.

On 13 June the team took-off from Culdrose for a full practice of its display routine. In good weather and clear visibility the team began their formation practice a mile off shore over Mounts Bay. During a turn, No 4 and No 6 aircraft collided, suffering fatal damage and crashed into the sea. The No 1 aircraft flown by the Team Leader, Lt-Cdr Alan Rock, was also severely damaged in the collision but was able to make an emergency landing in a field on a nearby clifftop where Lt-Cdr Rock and his passenger were treated for shock.

Within minutes of the accident, two Sea King and Wessex helicopters from Culdrose arrived over the scene. The Penlee and Porthleven lifeboats were launched and also joined the search of the area but it was clear at an early stage that there were no survivors amongst the two pilots and one passenger aboard the two Gazelles. The pilot of XX415, Ft Lt Robert Howley, whose award of the AFC had been announced in the Jubilee Honours list two days earlier, was on a two-year exchange posting and joined the team at the beginning of the season. His passenger was Lt-Cdr Geoffrey Bailey. The pilot of XW859 was Lt Paul Brown. All three crew were killed on impact.

The wreckage of the two Gazelles was located and recovered within days of the accident and during the subsequent technical investigation no evidence of any pre-accident malfunction was found in either aircraft.

This accident was untypical of most Royal Navy rotary wing accidents, since it occurred when six helicopters were practising aerobatic manoeuvres in very close formation at low level. Although all members of the team were highly experienced pilots, there remained little margin for error.

However, despite the fact that the team missed the remainder of the 1977 season, the Sharks reappeared the following year, now as a four-aircraft team, and have continued to entertain countless thousands at air displays up and down the country for the past 11 years without mishap. The Sharks are one of only two fulltime rotary wing formation teams in the world and are considered by the Royal Navy as an excellent showpiece for the professional skills of its pilots.

RN Sharks team seen in 1975 — their mid-air collision took place in 1977. *Royal Navy*

49

Date	Type	Serial	Unit	Location	Remarks
25/02	Jaguar GR1	XZ120	2 Sqn	Nordholm, Denmark	Crashed following loss of control
20/03	Wessex HU5	XS488	845 Sqn	Norway	Crashed from 20ft following whiteout
29/03	Chipmunk T10	WK515	1FWF	Nr Middle Wallop	Hit trees during unauthorised low flying
30/03	Wasp HAS1	XS531	703 Sqn	Nr Portland	Ditched in sea following loss of control on ship landing on HMS *Rothesay*
04/04	Buccaneer S2B	XW525	208 Sqn	Claerwen Reservoir, Wales	Crashed into reservoir following loss of tailplane when avoiding mid-air collision with two RAF Hunters
05/04	Wasp HAS1	XV637	–	13nm SW Plymouth	Ditched in the sea and sank while operating from HMS *Cleopatra*
26/04	Sea King HAS1	XV708	706 Sqn	–	Tailwheel collapsed during taxying; DBR
30/04	Jet Provost T5A	XW424	1FTS	Nr Linton-on-Ouse	Crashed during aerobatic practice
03/05	Canberra PR9	XH137	39 Sqn	RAF Wyton	Crashed during practice asymmetric overshoot; 5F
13/05	Hunter FGA9	XE651	TWU	40nm S Brawdy	Abandoned over sea following engine fire; Ej
17/05	Phantom FG1	XV588	892 Sqn	Nr Leuchars	Abandoned following engine fire on take-off; Ej
13/06	Gazelle HT2	XX415	705 Sqn	Mounts Bay, Cornwall	Mid-air collision with Gazelle (Sharks display team); 2F
13/06	Gazelle HT2	XW859	705 Sqn	Mounts Bay, Cornwall	Mid-air collision with Gazelle (Sharks display team); 1F
14/06	Jaguar GR1	XX978	31 Sqn	20nm SE Bremen, WG	Crashed following loss of control at low-level; 1F
29/07	Jaguar T2	XX148	226 OCU	Whittingham, Northumberland	Flew into ground; 2F
15/08	Canberra B6	WH948	100 Sqn	Nr Coltishall	Crashed following engine fire; Ej
18/08	Buccaneer S2B	XX890	15 Sqn	Nr Laarbruch, WG	Crashed on approach following loss of control
08/09	Hunter T7	XL571	TWU	Strumble Head	Abandoned following engine failure; Ej
29/09	Wasp HAS1	XT792	829 Sqn	Far East	Undercarriage collapse following heavy landing on HMS *Tiger* due to downdraught; DBR
24/10	Sea King HAS1	XV712	814 Sqn	South West Approaches	Hit deck during ship landing following tail pylon unlocked warning
25/10	Sea King HAS1	XV646	814 Sqn	South West Approaches	Ditched in sea following loss of control
31/10	Buccaneer S2	XV348	237 OCU	Glomfjord, Norway	Crashed following wirestrike; Ej; 1F
16/11	Jaguar T2	XX845	2 Sqn	Nr Laarbruch, WG	Belly landing

1978

Date	Type	Serial	Unit	Location	Cause
23/01	Jet Provost T5A	XW426	1FTS	Pickering, N Yorks	Crashed following failure to pull out of dive; 1F
30/01	Puma HC1	XW205	33 Sqn	Voss, Norway	Detached cabin door struck tail rotor; 1F
17/02	Gazelle AH1	XX404	657 Sqn	Armagh, NI	Lost control in high-speed turn; 2F
03/03	Gnat T1	XR981	CFS	RAF Kemble	Struck ground during practice aerobatics (Red Arrows); 2F
05/03	Chipmunk T10	WZ875	12 AEF	Loch Glow, Scotland	Flew into ground during aerobatics; 1F
21/03	Jaguar GR1	XX971	31 Sqn	Lahr, WG	Abandoned following engine failure on take-off; Ej
10/04	Scout AH1	XV132	655 Sqn	Lough Neath, NI	Crashed into lake following disorientation in snowstorm; 2F
26/04	Gnat T1	XR544	4FTS	RAF Valley	Crashed on approach
27/04	Jaguar T2	XX149	226 OCU	Cullin, Scotland	Flew into ground; 1F
12/05	Scout AH1	XP904	4 Flt	Lemgo, WG	Crashed following power failure
12/05	Phantom FG1	XT868	892 Sqn	–	Wing hit ground during practice display; Ej; 1F
13/05	Gazelle HT2	XX410	705 Sqn	Predannack	Crashed following loss of control; 2F
25/05	Hunter T8C	XF991	FRADU	Nr Yeovilton	Abandoned following engine explosion after take-off; Ej
25/05	Canberra PR9	XH176	A&AEE	Nr Chilmark, Wilts	Abandoned following loss of control on test flight; Ej
28/05	Beaver AL1	XV273	BATUS	Suffield, Canada	Crashed during downwind take-off
01/06	Jet Provost T3A	XN598	1FTS	Gouthwaite Reservoir, N Yorks	Wingtip hit water while flying low-level; 2F
14/06	Buccaneer S2A	XN975	RAE	Nr Oelde, WG	Abandoned following loss of control at low-level avoiding helicopter; Ej
18/06	Wessex HAS3	XP105	737 Sqn	Portsmouth	Ditched in sea after striking ship during low pass
19/06	Canberra B2	WJ753	100 Sqn	RAF Marham	Wingtip struck ground and cartwheeled; 3F
28/06	Jet Provost T5A	XW414	CFS	Nr Dishforth	Abandoned following engine seizure; Ej
05/07	Buccaneer S2A	XT285	RAE	West Freugh	Crashed on take-off; Tornado Dev; 1F
18/07	Wessex HAS3	XP105	737 Sqn	Nr Portsmouth	Controlled ditching near HMS *Devonshire*
24/07	Phantom FGR2	XV483	92 Sqn	Drenke, WG	Flew into ground during practice intercept; 2F
25/07	Jaguar GR1	XX823	17 Sqn	Off Sardinia	Crashed into hill following loss of control

Vulcan B2 XL390, 11 August 1978.
Crown Copyright

04/08	Wessex HU5	XS507	772 Sqn	Portland	Rolled over on ship landing following severe vibrations on lift-off
04/08	Phantom FGR2	XV403	111 Sqn	North Sea	Flew into sea during practice intercept
11/08	Vulcan B2	XL390	617 Sqn	Nr Glenview NAS, USA	Struck ground during flying display; 3F

Date	Type	Serial	Unit	Location	Cause
13/09	Wessex HAS3	XP110	737 Sqn	Off Portland Bill	Ditched in sea following engine failure
20/09	Wessex HAS3	XP143	737 Sqn	Nr Anglesey	Ditched in sea following engine surge
21/09	Bulldog T1	XX530	RN EFTS	Cockayne Ridge	Force-landing following engine failure; DBR
11/10	Gazelle AH1	XW869	ARWS	Nr Winchester	Struck ground following pilot distraction
01/11	Jaguar GR1	XX759	226 OCU	Nr Selkirk, Scotland	Crashed following loss of control; 1F (Ecuadorean pilot)
23/11	Phantom FG1	XT598	111 Sqn	Nr Leuchars	Flew into sea on approach; 2F
02/12	Scout AH1	XW614	–	NI	Crashed following NVG disorientation
07/12	Canberra PR7	WT530	13 Sqn	RAF Luqa, Malta	Crashed on take-off following loss of power from fuel contamination; DBR
15/12	Harrier GR3	XV801	3 Sqn	Eniegedoch, WG	Abandoned following loss of control; Ej

1979

Date	Type	Serial	Unit	Location	Cause
04/02	Wasp HAS1	XT441	829 Sqn	Off Gibraltar	Ditched in sea following engine fire; 1F
06/02	Gazelle AH1	XX377	3CBAS	Norway	Crashed during whiteout
08/02	Scout AH1	XW913	–	Netheravon	Crashed following inadvertent closure of fuel cock
08/02	Scout AH1	XR604	8 Flt	Hereford	Crashed on playing field
12/02	Gazelle AH1	XZ321	6 Flt	Gambia	Crashed following power failure due to fuel control unit
28/02	Phantom FG1	XV578	111 Sqn	North Sea off Scotland	Abandoned over sea following engine failure; Ej
06/03	Wessex HU5	XT465	846 Sqn	Nr Andoya, Norway	Crashed following wirestrike; 3F
14/03	Hunter F6	XJ637	1TWU	Talfarn, Wales	Abandoned following engine failure; Ej
26/03	Jaguar T2	XX147	17 Sqn	Sudljohn, WG	Abandoned following birdstrike; Ej
28/03	Jet Provost T3	XN585	1FTS	RAF Linton-on-Ouse	Abandoned following fire-warning on take-off; Ej
19/04	Wessex HC2	XR500	28 Sqn	Mirs Bay, HK	Struck water during winching practice in fog; DBR
19/04	Wessex HC2	XR500	28 Sqn	Off Hong Kong	Ditched in sea
22/05	Gnat T1	XP539	CFS	Nr Leeming	Abandoned following fuel blockage; Ej
25/05	Lightning F6	XS931	5 Sqn	Off Flamborough Head	Abandoned over sea after take-off following control restriction; Ej

The Red Arrows

Close formation flying dates back to World War 1 when British aircraft flew over enemy lines as close as possible for mutual protection. In 1920 the RAF's Central Flying School (CFS) combined the skills of aerobatic flying with close formation flying using a team of five Sopwith Snipes which made frequent appearances at major air displays in the immediate postwar years.

For the next 17 years, formation aerobatics, often with aircraft literally tied together, became a regular feature of the Hendon Pageants when they were performed by such RAF types as SE5s, Grebes, Siskins, Moths, Tutors, Bulldogs and the unforgettable Hawker Fury. The close-flying skills developed by the RAF during the 1930s were put to good use during World War 2 and the tradition was continued in peacetime with the establishment of the RAF's first jet team consisting of three Vampires in 1947. The Meteor replaced the Vampire in the early 1950s which in turn was replaced by the immortal Hunter five years later. The Hunter was for many the classic jet formation aircraft and it was used by teams of Nos 43 and 54 Squadrons and, in 1957, No 111 Squadron. The latter team, the first to appear using Hunters wearing anything other than camouflage, being painted high-gloss black overall, were naturally christened the 'Black Arrows', and thrilled air show crowds with their unique 22-Hunter loop. The 'Black Arrows' were replaced by another Hunter team, the 'Blue Diamonds' of No 92 Squadron in 1961. By this time the formation teams' displays had become choreographed to give a smooth flowing performance, aided by smoke and scripted commentaries.

Subtlety was replaced by the spectacle of power when the 'Tigers' and 'Firebirds' appeared at air shows using the mighty Lightning. However, the expense of maintaining a display team of high performance combat aircraft belonging to an operational fighter squadron soon became unacceptable and in 1964 the 'Red Pelicans' were formed, composed of six Jet Provost trainers from the CFS. They were joined by the 'Yellowjacks', made up of five of the RAF's latest agile advanced trainer, the Gnat T1, from No 4FTS based at RAF Valley, which in turn led to the formation of a new CFS team using the same type a year later.

Using nine distinctive red-painted Gnats, the team, christened the 'Red Arrows', became the RAF's first fulltime aerobatic team. Intensive training was carried out over the winter in preparation for the Red Arrows' first public appearance in May 1965 at the Biggin Hill International Air Fair. Success was immediate and 60 shows, including some in Europe, were flown in the first season.

By the end of 1970, the team was making more than 100 appearances a season, at which it had been seen by more than three million spectators and was the 'star' turn of television coverage of Farnborough, the Paris Air Show and the Biggin Hill Air Show. Each year, two or three 'new' pilots joined the Red Arrows to replace those at the end of what was usually a three-year tour with the team. During the intensive pre-season training at RAF Kemble, the team's base near Gloucester, new pilots have to be integrated into the team, new formations practised and the complete display programme finalised

Above right:
The main parachute deploys to drag the pilot of Hawk T1 XX251 clear of his disintegrating aircraft, 21 March 1984. *Crown Copyright*

Right:
Hawk T1 XX297 pictured at Scampton.
David Oliver

and polished to perfection before the AOC will allow it to be performed in public.

Between 1965 and 1971, the Arrows lost six aircraft due to a variety of causes, and all during the winter practice period. Three of the losses occurred during 1969; the first in March, when Gnat XR573 hit the ground at the bottom of a loop and was destroyed, and two others on the same day in December as the result of a misunderstanding when one of the team saw fire coming from the tailpipe of one of the Gnats during a formation practice. Unfortunately, two pilots, having both heard the fire warning and assumed that it was their aircraft on fire, left the formation and ejected. They suffered only minor injuries but both Gnats, XR992 and XR995, were destroyed as a result. A fourth Gnat, XR994, was lost in November 1970 when its pilot ejected during practice following an engine failure, but the team's most serious accident occurred two months later.

Two of the pilots who joined the Arrows during the winter of 1970 were Flt Lts Colin Armstrong and John Lewis. New team members often flew in the back seat of the Gnat with experienced pilots and during a routine practice on 20 January 1971, in preparation for a BBC television display, Armstrong and Lewis were being flown by Flt Lt Euan Perreaux, who had joined the team in 1969, and Flt Lt J. Haddock who had joined a year later, and who were the 'synchronised pair' duo for the coming season. One of the synchro pair's most popular and spectacular manoeuvres is called Roulette, a very low-level cross-over performed at a closing speed of 600mph. And it was whilst practising this manoeuvre at under 100ft over Kemble that the two Gnats, XR545 and XR986, collided in mid-air totally des-troying the aircraft and killing all four pilots. Almost immediately after the accident, the Team Leader, Sqn Ldr Loverseed, took the remainder of the team into the air for a practice flight.

Inevitably, following such an accident to a high profile unit like the Red Arrows, questions were asked in the House of Commons as to whether the team should be allowed to continue. The Secretary of State for Defence at that time was Lord Carrington who gave approval for the team to carry out a full display season, but with only seven aircraft and, pending the Board of Inquiry report, without the Roulette manoeuvre.

The Investigation established that neither aircraft suffered any mechanical fault and the cause of the accident was attributed to pilot error. Having under-gone a complete review of training and display procedures, particularly those of the synchro pair, the Arrows reverted to a nine-ship team which included a synchro pair, for the following season. Although the team was to lose three more Gnats in the next six years — all to mechanical failures — the Gnat-mounted Red Arrows were regarded by many as being the world's finest formation aerobatic team by the time it re-equipped with the RAF's new trainer, the BAe Hawk T1, at the end of the 1979 season.

Not only were the Red Arrows considered as a major recruiting tool by the RAF, but they had become an important public relations aid for the Service, and for British Aerospace. To exploit their position to the full, the team have had to squeeze ever more appearances into an already crowded schedule, leading to an even more crowded calendar. In recent years it has made extensive flag-waving visits to North America, the Middle East and the Far East. Despite the increased workload and long-range overseas flights, the team has been expected to maintain its own very high standards of performance and safety.

After 24 seasons and some 2,500 public performances, only two accidents have occurred during displays, neither of which caused any injuries to the pilots or the public. The first accident involving a Red Arrow Hawk, which incidentally was the first RAF Hawk loss, occurred during a display over the Brighton sea front on 17 May 1980. After breaking away from the main formation, the synchro pair began their series of low-level opposing passes. The display line chosen was over the sea, parallel to the coastline and between the Palace and West Piers. The show proceeded normally until the fourth 'opposition' pass by the pair at which point No 2 struck the mast of a yacht which, unnoticed, had motored slowly on to the previously clear display line. The yacht carried no sail at the time. The collision damaged the flying controls of the Hawk, which then rolled uncontrollably to the right. Just three seconds after the collision, with the aircraft almost inverted and at no more than 300ft above the sea, the pilot, Sqn Ldr Stephen Johnson, ejected. Although at the very limits of the seat's design parameters, the escape was successful and the pilot was quickly rescued by a motor boat, suffering only slight injuries. The Hawk, XX262, crashed in the sea beyond the Palace Pier.

After suffering a flame-out during practice, Hawk T1 XX297 crashed on approach to Scampton's Runway 23. *Lincolnshire Echo*

The authorised minimum height for the synchro pair at the time was 35ft. This height was safe given a clear range, whilst still providing a spectacle for the public. The display area between the pier was clear during the first part of the synchro pair display, but at the crucial moment the yacht, with a 44ft light grey mast and carrying no sail, moved into the display line. There was no embargo on boat movements during the display and therefore no reason for the skipper of the yacht to suspect that his passage would hazard the synchro pair. Its movement was neither anticipated nor noticed in time to warn the pilots. The pilot did not see the slow-moving obstruction against the vertical pier structure and the sea, and his aircraft struck the mast 4ft below its tip. In the circumstances, no blame was attached to the pilot. Immediately after the accident the minimum height for all Red Arrows displays was raised to 100ft. The rules and procedures for the team were again reviewed and foresight and vigilance, both in planning and on the spot control, were re-

Hawks XX241 and XX259 were both destroyed following a mid-air collision near the village of Melton, Lincs, on 16 November 1987.
Lincolnshire Echo

emphasised to avoid unexpected hazards.

The circumstances of the second display accident were more mundane. On the evening of 31 August 1984, the team was again performing over a sea front, this time at Sidmouth. As the main formation approached the top of a Vixen loop the pilot of No 8, Flt Lt Pete Lees, positioned on the rear righthand side of the main formation, experienced symptoms of a surge in the Adour engine of his aircraft. He attempted to regain control of the engine by carrying out all the necessary drills, but was unsuccessful and was therefore forced to eject. The Hawk, XX257, crashed into the sea some three miles off shore. Flt Lt Lees was rescued uninjured by the Sidmouth Inshore Rescue Boat about 5min after ejecting.

The Royal Navy mounted a salvage operation of the wreckage and the engine was recovered. Investigation of

it led the cause of the accident to be attributed to the failure of a blade in the low pressure compressor. The extensive damage to the compressor prevented the engine from being relit.

However, three pilots have lost their places in the Red Arrows as a result of accidents in the recent past. The first occurred on 21 March 1984 while the Arrows prepared for the first of a series

opposition loop — by the synchro pair. This procedure involves a head-on cross at a height of 100ft, a pull-up into a simultaneous loop to cross at the top in an inverted position, and a third cross-over during the final descent prior to achieving a 'crowd departure gate'. On this occasion it became apparent to both synchro pilots as they approached the top of the loop that Synchro 2 would

Red Arrows Hawk T1s used 1980-1990.

of full dress rehearsals which were to take place during the team's work-up detachment at RAF Akrotiri, Cyprus. Preparations included individual briefing of the synchro pair comprising Synchro 1 (the leader for synchronised aerobatics) and Synchro 2, Flt Lt Chris Hirst, who had been a team member since October 1982 and was preparing for his first synchro flying season. After take-off the display progressed normally until the final manoeuvre — the

be higher than Synchro 1 on the subsequent descent. To remedy this imbalance, Synchro 2 pulled more rapidly from the inverted position at the top of the loop and then relaxed his pull on the way down in order to gain speed on Synchro 1. As a result, when the third downward cross-over was achieved, Synchro 2 was in a steeper than usual attitude, although not alarmingly so. However, Synchro 2 continued to descend more steeply than Synchro 1 until at about 100ft above the airfield, and in spite of pulling the aircraft's nose up, the pilot was unable to prevent the Hawk, XX251, from striking the ground at high speed where it bounced several times.

During the initial impact the pilot's ejection seat was forced up its guide rails and through the canopy leaving Flt Lt Hirst exposed and in the airflow. The second impact forced the seat

downwards slightly and breached the seat firing mechanism, rendering it useless. By this stage, however, the forcible upward movement of the seat had triggered automatic man-seat separation devices so that, at the apogee of the aircraft's second bounce, the main parachute deployed to drag the pilot clear of the disintegrating Hawk and lower him quickly to the ground. The aircraft continued to a third and final impact where it broke up and caught fire. Flt Lt Hirst suffered abrasions, cuts and bruises which were later defined as major injuries.

After detailed investigation, it was concluded that the accident happened because the pilot had over-concentrated on achieving a good third cross-over without appreciating the flight-path he would have to follow in order to effect a safe recovery.

After the cross-over his immediate concerns had been to achieve a smoothly consistent smoke trail and a precise departure point. His proximity to the ground and the general geometry of the descent had been a lesser consideration until, having satisfied himself on the smoke trail aspects, he became fully aware of his predicament. By this time it was considered impossible to counter the Hawk's sink rate with the performance available.

Whilst the accident did not involve indiscipline or deliberate flouting of regulations, the team's activities were reviewed. Additional specialist briefings were also introduced to ensure that individual manoeuvres in the team's repertoire would be comprehensively considered once every two months during the work-up and display season. As a result of this accident, Flt Lt Hirst left the Red Arrows team, moving on to other duties within the RAF.

The most recent accident involving a Red Arrows Hawk (at the time of writing) happened once again during a practice, at the end of a long and exhausting display season, on 3 November 1986. During a practice over the Red Arrows' base (since 1982) at RAF Scampton in Lincolnshire, Red 8 suffered a flame-out and left the formation to attempt to relight the Adour and recover to the airfield. However, while initiating the standard relight procedures, the pilot of Hawk XX297, Flt Lt Dan Findlay, who had just completed his first season with the team, failed to appreciate how much height had been lost and was now extremely low on approach to Scampton's runway 23. In an effort to extend the approach, the pilot raised the nose but the aircraft hit the ground some way short of the threshold and Flt Lt Findlay ejected just before his aircraft crashed into a field and was destroyed.

Again, the investigation attributed the cause of the accident to an error by the pilot and again the team's activities and training procedures were reviewed.

Another accident occurred almost a year later and also resulted in one of the pilots involved having to leave the team, although for a different reason. At the end of the 1987 season Sqn Ldr Tim Miller, who had flown in the 1982-84 team, replaced Sqn Ldr Richard Thomas as Team Leader. On 16 November, Sqn Ldr Miller was leading a routine formation practice in the Scampton local area when, during a turn at 1,500ft, he called for airbrake. When Flt Lt Spike Newbery, who had joined the team at the end of 1986 — flying No 2 in line-astern — selected his airbrake, nothing happened. Despite pulling the power back, the No 2 slid under the leader and the two aircraft collided. The pilots immediately ejected but both suffered serious injuries. The Hawks, XX241 and XX259, were destroyed in the accident. One crashed in a field while the second fell on a row of houses in the village of Melton. Although some of the houses were occupied at the time no one was injured on the ground.

Sqn Ldr Miller recovered from his injuries and was able to lead the team in the 1988 season. Flt Lt Newbery's injuries, caused during the low-level and almost out-of-envelope ejection, were more serious and he was obliged to relinquish his place in the 1988 team on medical grounds.

It must be said that although the Red Arrows pilots are chosen for their above average flying abilities, they are still prone to making errors as much as any other experienced service pilot. Whilst the team's pilots undertake many hours of intensive practice in the skills of close formation aerobatics, they are also required to find time for normal continuation flying training which includes simulator time and emergency procedures training. The latter was reviewed in the light of the last Red Arrows accident and the frequency of non-formation flying training was increased as a result.

However, errors by Red Arrows pilots, who are seldom out of the public gaze, are rarely tolerated — even if they caused no danger to the public — and dismissal from the team often leads to the resignation from the Service of a very experienced pilot.

Despite the occasional accident, fewer on average than occur in most operational squadrons, the Red Arrows' safety record compares extremely favourably with every other major national formation team, few of which fly as many displays in a season. Twenty-five years after their formation, the Red Arrows are still considered by most as the world's premier flying display team.

Date	Type	Serial	Unit	Location	Description
25/05	Gazelle AH1	XX459	669 Sqn	Soltau, WG	Crashed after hitting power lines
07/06	Beaver AL1	XP805	BATUS	Suffield, Canada	Crashed on take-off following downdraught
12/06	Harrier GR3	XV781	3 Sqn	RAF Gutersloh	Abandoned during hover approach following fire: Ej
22/06	Jaguar T2	XX142	226 OCU	North Sea off Scotland	Flew into sea
03/07	Hunter FGA9	XK140	2TWU	Nr Lochives	Abandoned over sea following loss of control; Ej
03/07	Jet Provost T5A	XW371	7FTS	Nr Lancaster	Crashed during bad weather NAVEX; 1F
05/07	Lynx AH1	XZ189	1 Regt	Hildesheim, WG	Technical fault; 2F (First AAC Lynx accident)
06/07	Hunter F6	XG197	1TWU	Nr Tintagel, Cornwall	Abandoned over sea following engine failure; Ej
12/07	Buccaneer S2	XW526	16 Sqn	Nr Osnabruck, WG	Crashed following wing failure; 1F
18/07	Harrier GR3	XZ137	4 Sqn	Wissmar, WG	Crashed into houses
18/07	Jaguar GR1	XX960	14 Sqn	Iserlohn, WG	Abandoned following striking TV mast; Ej
07/08	Gazelle AH1	XW842	663 Sqn	Nr Soltau, WG	Crashed following wirestrike
15/08	Meteor D16	WH320	RAE Llanbedr	Aberporth Range	Shot down by Skyflash AAM from a 29 Sqn Phantom FGR2
17/08	Lightning F3	XP737	5 Sqn	Nr Valley	Abandoned over sea following u/c failure; Ej
24/08	Gazelle AH1	XZ293	662 Sqn	South Armagh, NI	Crashed following wirestrike; 1F
26/08	Scout AH1	XR601	BATUS	Suffield, Canada	Main rotor severed tail boom following heavy landing
01/09	Gazelle AH1	XX458	669 Sqn	Soltau, WG	Hit high ground during low flying
18/09	Lightning F6	XR723	5 Sqn	15nm S Akrotiri	Abandoned over sea following engine failure; Ej
21/09	Harrier GR3	XV757	1 Sqn	Wisbech, Cambs	Mid-air collision with XZ128; Ej; 3F (ground)
21/09	Harrier GR3	XZ128	1 Sqn	Wisbech, Cambs	Mid-air collision with XV757; Ej
29/09	Sea King HAS2	XZ673	-	-	Landed on ship with tail wheel over edge: DBR
04/10	Harrier GR3	XW766	3 Sqn	Ravensburg, WG	Abandoned following power loss; Ej
08/11	Harrier GR3	XV756	1 Sqn	Holbeach Range, Lincs	Crashed on to the beach following ricochet from own weapon; Ej
16/11	Bulldog T1	XX542	RNEFTS	Nr Leeming	Abandoned following loss of control in turbulence
23/11	Jaguar GR1	XX762	226 OCU	Nr Lossiemouth	Crashed into mountain during low-level exercise; 1F
25/11	Sioux AH1	XT845	1 Wing	WG	Crashed in woods
10/12	Jaguar GR1	XX749	226 OCU	Nr Lumsden, Scotland	Mid-air collision during formation turn; 1F
10/12	Jaguar GR1	XX755	226 OCU	Nr Lumsden, Scotland	Mid-air collision; Ej
27/12	Puma HC1	XW228	33 Sqn	Mtoko, Rhodesia	Struck telegraph pole; DBR

Left:
Hunter F6A XG197, 6 July 1979.
Crown Copyright

Below:
Puma HC1 XW228, 27 December 1979.
Crown Copyright

Below:
Lightning F6 XR723 about to take off from Akrotiri on its last flight, on 18 September 1979. *Avia Press*

64

Date	Type	Serial	Unit	Location	Cause
14/01	Beaver AL1	XP819	Beaver Flt	Basingstoke, Hants	Crashed in open ground in thick fog
15/01	Sea King HAS2	XZ572	814 Sqn	Off Florida, USA	Ditched in sea following oil leak
07/02	Buccaneer S2A	XV345	15 Sqn	Nr Nellis AFB, USA	Broke up in low-level flight during 'Red Flag' exercise; 2F
12/02	Hunter FGA9	XK151	2 TWU	Isle of Skye	Crashed into high ground during low-level flight; 1F
18/02	Gazelle AH1	XZ306	651 Sqn	Nr Lisburn, NI	Crashed following wirestrike; 1F
05/03	Phantom FGR2	XV436	29 Sqn	RAF Coningsby	Crashed on landing following flapless landing at night and missing cable
12/03	Harrier GR3	XW765	3 Sqn	Nr Gutersloh, WG	Abandoned following birdstrike; Ej
08/05	Jet Provost T5A	XW314	RAFC	Nr Cranwell	Crashed on approach following loss of control during spin training; Ej
08/05	Whirlwind HAR10	XN127	CFS	RAF Shawbury	Uncontrolled rolling drive into ground; F
16/05	Pembroke C1	XL953	60 Sqn	RAF Wildenrath, WG	Ground fire
17/05	Hawk T1	XX262	CFS	Brighton seafront	Abandoned after hitting yacht mast during aerobatic display (Red Arrows); Ej
22/05	Wessex HU5	XT763	772 Sqn	Weymouth Bay	Ditched in sea following loss of transmission oil pressure
28/05	Hunter FGA9	XG261	2TWU	Nr Dufftown, Scotland	Abandoned following loss of control during low-level combat training; Ej
28/05	Jaguar GR1	XX961	17 Sqn	RAF Bruggen, WG	Mid-air collision during break from arrow formation; 1F
28/05	Jaguar GR1	XX964	17 Sqn	RAF Bruggen, WG	Mid-air collision during break from arrow formation; Ej
29/05	Hunter T7	XL597	216 Sqn	Nr Little Saxham	Abandoned following engine explosion; Ej
03/06	Phantom FG1	XV589	111 Sqn	RAF Alconbury	Abandoned on approach following radome opening; Ej
10/06	Gazelle AH1	XX390	3CBAS	Lough Foyle, NI	Crashed into water while low-flying
27/06	Wessex HAS3	XP156	737 Sqn	Off Portland	Crashed into sea; 4F
11/07	Phantom FGR2	XV589	92 Sqn	Nr Diepholz, WG	Flew into ground during BBC filming sortie; 2F
17/07	Jaguar GR1	XX817	17 Sqn	RAF Bruggen, WG	Abandoned on approach following engine fire; Ej

3 June 1980: Phantom FGR1 XV589

Circumstances:
Phantom FGR1 XV589 detached from RAF Leuchars for training purposes, was flying a routine sortie from RAF Alconbury. The flight had proceeded as planned and the aircraft positioned for landing. As it reached 350ft above the ground and lined up for the runway, the nose section radome was seen to open slightly, close, open again and then fold back on its hinge until it lay against the right hand side of the fuselage facing backwards. This resulted in sudden asymmetric drag which caused the aircraft to roll and yaw to the right. The pilot attempted to correct this without success. As the aircraft lost height and continued to roll out of control, the pilot realised that abandonment was the only course remaining. He therefore ejected and the navigator followed almost immediately. Both members of the crew landed safely and virtually uninjured. The aircraft crashed in a field short of the runway and was destroyed.

Cause:
The radome had been correctly closed and locked before flight, the locking device had been physically checked by groundcrew and the pilot, and nothing untoward was seen by qualified observers using binoculars from van-tage points before the aircraft took off. The sortie included manoeuvres involving 'g' forces from 0-6, and until the final approach the radome remained closed. The locking device was recovered from the wreckage; there was no sign of structural failure or metal fatigue but there was seen to be a considerable amount of wear between the locking bolt and its receptacle, and some looseness in the handle used to open and close the radome. This was the result of frequent use over many years. Similar wear was found on a number of other aircraft and it was concluded that it would be possible for the radome to become unlocked in flight by a combination of acceleration, of 'g' forces, aerodynamic loads and vibration.

Subsequent actions:
All Phantoms with a similar radome locking system have been inspected for excessive wear. The mechanism is being modified to provide a more secure locking device and engineering procedures have been amended to ensure regular inspection for wear and correct adjustment.

XV589 of No 111 Squadron. *MAP*

17 Nov 1980: Nimrod MR2/XV256

Circumstances:

Just before 07.30hrs on 17 November 1980, a crew took off from RAF Kinloss in semi-darkness on a final sortie of their conversion from the Nimrod MR1 to the MR2. Being the final sortie, the normal crew was increased to 20 by five checking crew and an additional Air Engineer. The surface wind was 07°-02kt with 8km visibility in rain and a main cloud base of 3,000ft. Engine response and indications during the take-off run were normal but shortly after take-off, at an estimated height of 20ft, the aircraft flew through a dense flock of sea birds and suffered numerous bird-strikes. Almost simultaneously the No 1 engine surged violently, suffering a catastrophic internal failure. The low pressure compressors on the No 2 and 3 engines were also damaged and, although they continued to run, they produced little thrust. Effectively the fully-laden aircraft was being powered by only No 4 engine which itself may have been damaged.

The captain, an RAAF exchange pilot, endeavoured to maintain what little height and speed he had by ordering full power on the live engines and raising the undercarriage. However, with only limited power available he was soon faced with no alternative but to attempt a controlled crash-landing. Some 27sec after take-off the aircraft came down on relatively soft tree-tops of a forest area 1,300yd from the end of the runway and was quickly engulfed in flames. Eighteen crew members managed to evacuate the wrecked and burning aircraft but both the pilot and co-pilot were killed. The aircraft was destroyed.

Cause:

The investigation into the accident established that the cause was a multiple bird strike which occurred at a critical stage of flight. The aircraft suffered such a loss of thrust that maintenance of height and speed quickly became impossible. It was the captain's skill in keeping the stricken aircraft airborne long enough to make a smooth and controlled crash at minimum speed into tree-tops that undoubtedly saved the lives of 18 crew members. After the accident, 77 dead sea birds were found on or near the runway. It is known that many others were ingested in the engines.

The captain called the crew to crash stations and, despite the short time available, the crew members were able to respond and brace themselves before impact. There was considerable bumping and jolting as the aircraft went through the trees but the deceleration was insufficient to initiate the inertia crash switches – the emergency lights did not come on nor did the fire bottles discharge. However, the normal cabin lights stayed on for a short while after impact, together with the locking indication lights for sonobuoy fixed launchers, and illumination was provided by the flames outside.

Early in the emergency the captain had warned the crew that he might have to ditch and this, together with the relatively slow speed deceleration, initially caused some confusion. Although shocked and dazed, the crew started to evacuate the aircraft as soon as it came to rest, only to find that they had not ditched in the water but were surrounded by blazing forest. Inside the fuselage conditions were appalling. The protruding beam windows had broken during the crash and burning fuel had entered through the starboard window, burning a crew member's flying suit. Heat had caused the decomposition of the PVC sheeting laced over the cabin sound-proofing material so that volumes of dense acrid smoke rapidly built

Nimrod MR2 XV256, 17 November 1980.
Crown Copyright

up making conditions intolerable within 2min.

Various articles, such as documents, galley equipment and hand-held fire extinguishers, were thrown forward during impact. The removable floor panels covering access to the hydraulic, aileron and elevator bays, broke free leaving large holes in the floor which considerably hindered movement inside the aircraft. At least one crew member stumbled into such a hole as he searched for an escape route.

In these terrible conditions most of the crew made their way rearwards where, after some difficulty with the starboard door, both entrance doors were opened but the way seemed blocked by flames. In the ever worsening situation some of the crew started to move forward again but quickly realised that the flames would have to be braved. Despite the many hazards in the burning, smoke-filled fuselage, 18 crew members escaped — 12 through the port rear entrance door, one through the starboard overwing escape hatch, two via the starboard front door and three via the broken beam windows. Of those who used the beam windows, one had suffered a broken leg in the impact when the fuselage side wall hit a tree and another stuck halfway through the hole and had to be dragged clear by a crew member who had already cleared the wreckage. Other injuries consisted of one crew member who had suffered bruising to a leg and a bruise to his head, and two who had slight burns. All the survivors suffered from smoke inhalation.

Not surprisingly, the front of the aircraft bore the brunt of the impact. Because conventional protective helmets are unsuitable for Nimrod operations, the pilots were not wearing them and they both received blows to the head causing severe injuries which completely incapacitated them. The rapidly deteriorating conditions both inside and outside the fuselage made their rescue impossible.

Subsequent actions:
This was the first Nimrod major accident in over 11 years of service and was caused by a massive bird strike.

The methods of bird control used at Kinloss are standard and have been reviewed several times without any-

thing suggesting a need for change. Prior to every aircraft movement an airfield search for birds is made and on this occasion the search, made in semi-darkness, did not reveal any roosting birds.

To reduce the bird hazard further, Kinloss airfield drainage has been improved, much reducing the amount of standing water which would otherwise make the airfield attractive to particular species.

Three other measures are being pursued. First, the Institute of Medicine is investigating the possibility of designing a comfortable lightweight head protection suitable for use in Nimrods. Second, the loose article hazard is being examined and steps are being taken to improve the security of such things as floor access panels. Finally, the major hazard presented by the rapid build-up of smoke will be lessened as the lagging material around the sound-proofing of Nimrods is replaced with an improved type.

Claims:
A claim was received from the Forestry Commission in respect of damage to trees and it has been settled.

Nimrod MR1 XV256 which crashed at RAF Kinloss following a multiple birdstrike. *MAP*

Date	Type	Serial	Unit	Location	Cause
31/07	Jet Provost T3A	XN590	RAFC	RAF Elvington	Birdstrike on take-off
14/08	Scout AH1	XP908	660 Sqn	New Territories, HK	Force-landing following tail rotor strike; overloaded
19/08	Hawk T1	XX243	4FTS	RAF Valley	Crashed after landing following collision with ground emplacement; DBR
15/09	Gazelle AH1	XX401	3CBAS	HMS *Intrepid*, Balnakiel, Scotland	Crashed during Exercise 'Teamwork 80'; 3F
18/09	Bulldog T1	XX545	London UAS	RAF Abingdon	Abandoned following simulated engine failure
14/10	Harrier GR3	XV792	3 Sqn	RAF Gutersloh, WG	Crashed on hover approach following uncontrollable roll
28/10	Harrier GR3	XV761	4 Sqn	Nr Bitburg, WG	Abandoned following loss of power following bird ingestion; Ej
07/11	Canberra B2	WH667	100 Sqn	RAF Akrotiri, Cyprus	Crashed on take-off following engine explosion; 2F
11/11	Chipmunk T10	XP972	BFWF	Middle Wallop	Crashed following power loss during take-off
12/11	Phantom FGR2	XV413	29 Sqn	50nm NE Cromer	Crashed into sea at night; 2F
17/11	Nimrod MR2	XV256		RAF Kinloss	Crashed on overshoot following multiple birdstrike; 2F
18/11	Gazelle HT3	ZA801	CFS	Chetwynd airfield, Salop	Crashed during turn following loss of control; DBR
01/12	Sea Harrier FRS1	XZ454	800 Sqn	Nr Lizard, Cornwall	Ditched in sea after hitting ramp following high rate of sink on deck landing; Ej
09/12	Phantom FGR2	XV414	23 Sqn	10nm NE Lowestoft	Abandoned over sea following engine fire; Ej

1981

Date	Type	Serial	Unit	Location	Cause
20/01	Sea King HAS2A	XV665	829 Sqn	Persian Gulf	Ditched in sea following tail rotor drive failure
28/01	Jet Provost T5A	XW308	1FTS	Nr Kilmarny, Fife	Crashed in field during solo NAVEX; 1F
12/02	Jaguar GR1	XX827	17 Sqn	Nellis Range, Neveda, USA	Hit ground during low-level 'Red Flag' sortie; 1F
18/02	Sea King HAS2	XV701	806 Sqn	Nr Helford	Ditched at sea following loss of control in hover
23/02	Hunter FGA9	XE552	2TWU	Nr Lossiemouth	Crashed into sea; 1F
06/03	Sea King HAS2	XZ915	820 Sqn	Isle of Wight	Mid-air collision, crashed into sea; 3F
06/03	Sea King HAS2	XZ917	820 Sqn	Isle of Wight	Mid-air collision, crashed into sea; 2F

Date	Type	Serial	Unit	Location	Remarks
11/03	Wessex HAS3	XM872	737 Sqn	Nr Portland	Ditched in sea following engine fire
17/03	Hunter GA11	XF977	FRADU	Nr Start Point	Abandoned over sea following engine failure during low-level pass; Ej
27/03	Lightning T5	XS459	LTF	Nr Binbrook	Crashed on approach
03/04	Hunter FGA9	XG151	2TWU	RAF Lossiemouth	Abandoned on finals following flame-out; Ej
14/04	Jaguar GR1	XX973	31 Sqn	Nr Gutersloh	Abandoned following spin; Ej
23/05	Wessex HU5	–	772 Sqn	Nr Portland	Ditched in sea
26/05	Harrier GR5	XW923	1417 Flt	Belize	Abandoned following loss of control during short take-off; Ej
01/06	Bulldog T1	XX514	RNEFTS	Nr Leeming	
01/06	Jaguar T2	XX828	226 OCU	Nr Forfar, Scotland	Crashed following birdstrike; Ej
03/06	Whirlwind HAR10	XP347	RAFG	Nr Koksijde, Belgium	Crashed on landing following failure of tail rotor drive; DBR
16/06	Jet Provost	XW329	3FTS	RAF Leeming	Stalled on practice turnback after take-off
28/06	Wessex HAS3	XP156	737 Sqn	Nr Portland	Crashed into sea; 3F
30/06	Lynx AH1	XZ182	654 Sqn	Nr Hildersheim, WG	–
30/06	Gazelle HT1	XX396	2FTS	RAF Shawbury	Heavy landing, tail struck ground, DBR
09/07	Wessex HU5	XT448	845 Sqn	Nr Savannah, USA	Ditched in sea
09/07	Phantom FG1	XT866	43 Sqn	RAF Leuchars	Abandoned on finals followng ADI failure at night; Ej
14/07	Harrier GR3	XV807	1417 Flt	Nr Georgeville, Belize	Loss of control following tailplane link disconnected; Ej
15/07	Wessex HAS3	XP118	737 Sqn	Channel	Ditched in sea following engine run down
17/07	Jaguar GR1	XX113	226 OCU	Nr Gt Malvern	Abandoned following loss of control; Ej
17/07	Jaguar GR1	XX817	–	RAF Bruggen, WG	Abandoned on approach following engine fire; Ej
23/07	Lightning F6	XR765	5 Sqn	50nm NNE Binbrook	Abandoned over the sea following engine fire; Ej
24/07	Jaguar T2	XX916	ETPS	Bristol Channel	Crashed into sea
30/07	Jet Provost T3	XN643	1FTS	Snainton, N Yorks	Abandoned following flame-out during aerobatics; Ej
06/08	Jaguar GR1	XX972	31 Sqn	Barnard Castle, Scotland	Crashed into ground during low-level flight; 1F
25/08	Harrier GR3	XZ139	3 Sqn	Nr Alhorn, WG	Abandoned following tailplane linkage failure; Ej
23/09	Buccaneer S2	XW537	237 OCU	RAF Wattisham	Stalled on approach; Ej
07/10	Wessex HU5	XT448	–	–	Ditched in sea following loss of tail rotor control

28 Jan 1981: Jet Provost T5A XW308

Circumstances:
The pilot, from RAF Linton-on-Ouse, was a student undergoing navigation training in Scotland, as part of a detachment which had been prompted by the forecast of poor weather at his base in the Vale of York. During the morning of 28 January 1981 he was briefed to fly a low-level navigation sortie from RAF Leuchars to another airfield, refuel, and return at high-level the same day. The weather at Leuchars when the student pilot took-off was 2/8 cloud cover at 700ft increasing to complete cover at 1,000ft with cloud reported as varying between 2,600 and 5,000ft. Visibility was 10km in smoke (light haze). The student pilot took off at midday from Runway 27, climbed straight ahead as briefed, changed to the Approach frequency at about 700ft by manually dialling it and entered cloud at an estimated height of 1,000ft. He requested and was given clearance to turn right on to a heading of 035°. He acknowledged this and the Regional Pressure Setting (RPS). This was his last transmission. The aircraft was next seen exiting cloud in a near vertical descent. Fractionally later another eyewitness saw the aircraft fly in a NE direction in a level flight attitude but banked to the right. Seconds later the aircraft crashed into a wheat field on the lower slopes of a hill 1min 43sec after take-off. The student pilot made no attempt to eject and was killed instantly. The aircraft was destroyed.

Cause:
The cause of the accident cannot be precisely determined. However, it seems likely that after acknowledging the RPS and clearance to turn, the pilot initiated a turn to the right while still in cloud. Having set the RPS on the main altimeter, the position that the compass pointer was found in (010°) suggests he started to move it on to 035°, his intended heading. This action required a change of hands on the control column and he may have been distracted from his instruments. The aircraft went into a steep spiral dive and the pilot possibly blacked out under the 'g' forces exerted as he tried to correct the loss of height. However, shortly after emerging from cloud, evidence suggests that he started to roll the wings level and recover from the dive, but it was too late to avoid hitting the ground. Although it is clear that the aircraft went out of control, it is stressed that the presumed sequence set out above is conjecture and the exact chain of causation cannot be determined.

Claims:
A claim for damage of crops has been settled.

XW308, a Jet Provost T5A of No 1FTS, crashed on 28 January 1981. *MAP*

Date	Type	Serial	Unit	Location	Cause
21/10	Jaguar GR1	XX957	20 Sqn	RAF Bruggen, WG	Lightning strike on approach; Ej
21/10	Hunter T7	XL619	1TWU	50nm SW Brawdy	Abandoned following loss of control during inverted spin; Ej
22/10	Jet Provost T3	XM366	7FTS	Holme-on-Spalding Moor	Abandoned following flame-out; Ej
18/11	Jaguar GR1	XX758	226 OCU	Nr Dingwall, Scotland	Flew into high ground during low-level flight; 1F
01/12	Hunter T7	XL583	1TWU	RAF Brawdy	Abandoned on finals following engine failure; Ej
13/12	Wasp HAS1	XT418	829 Sqn	Falkland Is	Roll over on beach landing following windshear on approach

1982

Date	Type	Serial	Unit	Location	Cause
07/01	Hawk T1	XX344	MoD(PE)	RAE Bedford	Crashed on landing due to wake turbulence; Ej
12/02	Harrier GR3	XZ973	233 OCU	Berwy Hill, N Wales	Crashed into high ground during low-level flight (USAF pilot); 1F
20/02	Bulldog T1	XX662	Edinburgh UAS	Nr Neacham	Abandoned following uncontrollable spin; Ej
22/02	Harvard T2B	KF314	MoD(PE)	Nr Chilmark, Wilts	Crashed into ground following a spin; 2F
24/02	Gazelle AH1	XW905	AAC	Voss, Norway	Whiteout; 3I
24/02	Gazelle AH1	XX378	AAC	Voss, Norway	Whiteout
25/02	Canberra B2	WK116	100 Sqn	RAF Akrotiri, Cyprus	Abandoned following double flame-out on take-off; Ej
08/03	Buccaneer S2B	XN977	15 Sqn	RAF Laarbruch, WG	Crashed on landing; DBR
12/03	Gazelle HT2	XX397	705 Sqn	Nr Goonhilly	Struck ground during recovery from wingover
17/03	Hunter T7	–	RAE	Farnborough	Abandoned following engine explosion on take-off; Ej
02/04	Jaguar GR1	XX122	54 Sqn	The Wash	Crashed into sea on range (Norwegian pilot); 1F
14/04	Phantom FGR2	XT912	228 OCU	Walcot, Lincs	Mid-air collision at low-level after take-off; Ej
22/04	Jet Provost T4	XP564	1TWU	Nant-Y-Moch Reservoir	Abandoned following throttle linkage breakage; Ej
22/04	Wessex HU5	XT464	845 Sqn	Fortuna Glacier, South Georgia	Whiteout after take-off

Date	Type	Serial	Squadron	Location	Remarks
22/04	Wessex HU5	XT473	845 Sqn	Fortuna Glacier, South Georgia	Whiteout after take-off
24/04	Sea King HC4	ZA311	846 Sqn	HMS *Hermes*, South Atlantic	Ditched in sea; 1F
04/05	Sea Harrier FRS1	XZ450	899 Sqn	Goose Green, Falkland Is	Shot down by Argentine AA guns; 1F
06/05	Sea Harrier FRS1	XZ452	801 Sqn	HMS *Invincible*, South Atlantic	Mid-air collision over sea; 1F
06/05	Sea Harrier FRS1	XZ453	801 Sqn	HMS *Invincible*, South Atlantic	Mid-air collision over sea; 1F
12/05	Sea King HAS5	ZA132	826 Sqn;	HMS *Hermes*, South Atlantic	Ditched in sea
13/05	Hunter FGA9	XE649	1TWU	Nr Aberystwyth	Abandoned following engine fire; Ej
17/05	Sea Harrier FRS1	XZ438	899 Sqn	RNAS Yeovilton	Abandoned following failure to become airborne; Ej
17/05	Jet Provost T5A	XW288	1FTS	Nr Linton	Crashed during low-level aerobatics; 1F
18/05	Sea King HAS5	XZ573	826 Sqn	HMS *Invincible*, South Atlantic	Ditched in sea
19/05	Sea King HC4	ZA290	846 Sqn	Punta Arenas, Chile	Burnt by crew during covert operation
20/05	Sea King HC4	ZA294	864 Sqn	HMS *Hermes*, South Atlantic	Ditched in sea at night; 21F
21/05	Harrier GR3	XZ972	1 Sqn	Port Howard, Falkland Is	Shot down by Argentine Blowpipe SAM; Ej
21/05	Gazelle AH1	XX402	3CBAS	San Carlos, Falkland Is	Shot down by Argentine small-arms fire: 2F
21/05	Gazelle AH1	XX411	3CBAS	San Carlos, Falkland Is	Ditched in sea after being hit by Argentine small-arms fire
21/05	Lynx HAS2	XZ251	815 Sqn	HMS *Ardent*, South Atlantic	Destroyed by Argentine bomb during the sinking of *Ardent*
23/05	Chipmunk T10	WP979	5AEF	Nr Cambridge Airport	Crashed in circuit following pilot incapacitation
24/05	Sea Harrier FRS1	ZA192	899 Sqn	Stanley Airport, Falkland Is	Shot down by Argentine AA guns; 1F
25/05	Jaguar GR1	XX963	14 Sqn	Nr Wesel WG	Shot down by Sidewinder accidentally fired from RAF Phantom; Ej
25/05	Wessex HU5	XS480	848 Sqn	*Atlantic Conveyor*, South Atlantic	Lost during sinking of *Atlantic Conveyor* by Argentine Exocet missile
25/05	Wessex HU5	XS495	848 Sqn	*Atlantic Conveyor*, South Atlantic	Lost during sinking of *Atlantic Conveyor* by Argentine Exocet missile
25/05	Wessex HU5	XS499	848 Sqn	*Atlantic Conveyor*, South Atlantic	Lost during sinking of *Atlantic Conveyor* by Argentine Exocet missile

6 June 1982: Gazelle AH1 XX377

Gazelle AH1 XX377 was originally on the strength of 3 CBAS (3rd Commando Brigade Squadron) but reallocated to No 656 Squadron on sailing for the Falklands aboard *Nordic Ferry* on 9 May 1982. It arrived at San Carlos on 3 June.

On 6 June XX377 was tasked to take spares and fuel from Darwin to Mount Pleasant where a REBRO (Relay Broadcast) Station had become unserviceable. Whilst some two miles from the peak, flying at between 70 and 200ft AGL in bad weather and poor visibility, the Gazelle was hit by a Sea Dart missile fired from the destroyer, HMS *Cardiff*.

XX377 crashed immediately and was destroyed. All four occupants, SSgt Christopher Griffin, pilot; LCpl Simon Cockton, aircrewman; Maj Michael Forge, Signals Sqn CO; and SSgt John Baker Signals Sqn, were killed on impact, HMS *Cardiff* was reported to have fired two Sea Darts early on 6 June at unidentified and slow-moving aircraft heading east towards Fitzroy settlement, but no hits were confirmed. The destroyer's commander had been told that the targets were in an area in which there would be no 'friendly' aircraft operating.

Below:
HMS *Cardiff* was involved in the Gazelle shoot-down in the Falklands. *David Oliver*

Right:
HMS *Cardiff's* Sea Dart anti-aircraft missile launcher. *David Oliver*

7 Jan 1982: Hawk T1

Circumstances:
On completion of a sortie the Hawk joined the circuit at RAE Bedford for landing. The surface wind was easterly at about 6kt, giving light tailwind and crosswind components for landing. A Britannia aircraft, already in the circuit, was cleared for a roller landing ahead of the Hawk. The Britannia made a normal approach and touchdown before rolling and as it climbed away the Hawk was cleared to land. On the final approach to land, at a height of about 20ft over the runway threshold, the Hawk was seen to roll progressively to the right, apparently out of control. The pilot ejected as the angle of bank approached 90° but the navigator made no attempt to eject.

The aircraft struck the ground starboard wingtip first then rolled on to its back and slid along the runway some 1,200ft. The pilot impacted on the ground still in his seat and before the parachute had time to deploy. The navigator, still strapped into his seat in the aircraft, had his protective helmet worn through to the inner fabric as the aircraft slid along the ground on its back. The aircraft was damaged beyond repair.

The crash rescue services were quickly on the scene and, in extremely difficult circumstances, made a well co-ordinated, timely and strenuous effort to extract the navigator from the wreckage. Five firemen received bravery awards for their part in the rescue and one fireman in particular displayed a dedication to duty and bravery in the highest traditions of the Fire Service. With the rear ejection seat damaged and in an unknown state of safety and the possibility that the seat, rocket pack or drogue gun might fire at any time, he unhesitatingly went to the assistance of the injured navigator and was inside the damaged rear cockpit for about 15min, including when the aircraft was lifted by crane just sufficient to extract the navigator.

Cause:
Both pilot and navigator were concussed and suffered memory loss, and could not recall the accident or the events immediately preceding it. After investigating all possible causes including control restriction, trim runaway, mishandling, birdstrike, icing, asymmetric flap, engine failure and structural failure, it was determined that the accident occurred when the Hawk flew into a wingtip vortex shed by the Britannia flying about 45sec and 9,000ft ahead of the Hawk. This theory was verified by flight test measurement of a Britannia vortex which, in the circumstances pertaining at the time of the accident could have induced rolling moments about 2.8 times the available roll control of the Hawk at approach conditions.

The pilot ejected when the aircraft attained an attitude from which he apparently considered recovery was unlikely before the aircraft hit the ground. His action in this respect was entirely correct and in accordance with standard procedure for such circumstances when a crash is imminent. The fact that the navigator stayed in the aircraft probably saved his life as the aircraft was by then well outside the safe ejection envelope.

Subsequent action:
The circumstances of the accident have been widely publicised throughout the Services and elsewhere. The accident highlights the strength of wake turbulence from medium/heavy aircraft — even at a separation of 9,000ft — and also the increased risk of wake turbulence persisting at the runway threshold in light wind conditions.

The British Aerospace Hawk T1. *BAe*

22 Feb 1982: Harvard T2B KF314

Circumstances:

The MOD(PE) Harvard took off from Boscombe Down on a flight to renew the second pilot's currency on type. The weather was good and entirely suitable for the flight. After take-off the aircraft climbed to the west and a height of about 8,000ft, called Boscombe Down Air Traffic Control to say they would be spinning as planned in 30sec. This was the last known radio transmission from the aircraft. Five minutes later Air Traffic Control became aware that the Harvard had disappeared from radar contact and, having failed to re-establish radio contact, vectored a helicopter to the last known position of the aircraft. A few minutes later the

helicopter crew saw the wreckage of the Harvard in a field, landed alongside and subsequently reported that there were no survivors.

The aircraft was destroyed. Analysis of ground radar recordings shows that the Harvard carried out one spin and recovery followed by another spiral-type manoeuvre, probably a spin, and recovered to apparently normal flight appreciably above the lower limit of radar cover. The aircraft was subsequently seen and heard by a number of ground witnesses who reported seeing it in a turn at 500ft, then commenced a descent to low level on a northerly heading before turning into a righthand almost illiptical circuit. When

80

on a southwesterly heading the nose went up and the aircraft climbed steeply, then the wing dropped quickly, possibly in a stall, before the aircraft dived steeply to the ground. No attempt was made by the crew to abandon the aircraft.

Cause:
Despite a lengthy and comprehensive investigation, no cause of the accident has been established. There was no toxicological or pre-existing medical condition likely to have incapacitated either pilot. Various theories were advanced on possible control or engine malfunctions and, although there was some evidence to suggest either possi-

bility, none was supported by sufficient evidence to warrant description as a probable cause of the accident. There remains the far more remote possibility that some factor lost in the crash led to this accident.

Subsequent action:
As a precautionary measure the Harvard structural survey schedule was reviewed to assess the possible need for additional checks and the servicing schedules were reviewed for thoroughness and periodicity, particularly in regard to the engine and flying control systems. Minor amendments have since been made to the schedules. It should be emphasised that the Harvard has had an exceptionally long history as a successful and safe training aircraft. The investigation into this accident, although inconclusive, has not uncovered anything to suggest that any form of restriction should be put on the aircraft.

Harvard T2B KF314 which crashed following a spin, 22 February 1982.

20 Sep 1982: Buccaneer S2B XV160

Circumstances:
Buccaneer XV160 was one of a number of aircraft detached to Deccimomannu airfield in Sardinia to enable aircrew to practice weapon deliveries on Capo Frasca range. On 20 September 1982, the aircraft was flown by an experienced pilot, though one relatively new to the Buccaneer and its role, accompanied by an experienced navigator. The sortie was designed to practise several types of attack, the first three of which were entirely successful. The fourth was to be a visual computer-directed bombing attack, with an automatic weapon release during a programmed and steep climb from low-level. During the ensuing climb by the pilot, following the indications of his computer, the navigator prepared the weapons system and counted down to expected bomb release.

At this stage, the pilot heard the aircraft's stalling warning system signalling that his aircraft was about to stall. Moments later the aircraft went out of control, rolled sharply right and then left, and eventually descended flatly and slowly. Meanwhile the pilot applied anti-spin controls, but the aircraft did not respond and, at an indicated height of 4,000ft, with the aircraft still out of control, the pilot ejected, followed immediately by his navigator. Both crew landed safely, although the pilot suffered a spinal injury. The aircraft crashed into the edge of cliffs short of the target area and was destroyed.

Cause:
It was established that no pre-impact structural failure had occurred. Although some parts of the aircraft and its systems could not be recovered for specialist examination, the likelihood of any technical failure having contributed to the accident was considered to have been remote. It was concluded that the aircraft had probably pulled-up more sharply than usual, which resulted in a lower airspeed than normal at weapon release and a correspondingly higher angle of climb. Smooth careful handling would have ensured a safe recovery. However, the margin for error was small and the pilot's instinctive attempt to recover from the attack when he heard the stall warning was thought to have precipitated autorotation, resulting in the loss of control. It was confirmed that there had been insufficient height available to regain controlled flight once the aircraft had stalled.

The Buccaneer S2B.

May 1982 was memorable for being the month in which British Forces landed in the Falkland Islands following the Argentine invasion, and when reports of aircraft being shot down by British Sidewinder air-to-air missiles were making daily headline news.

However, what at first sight appeared to be an erroneous headline on 25 May announcing that an RAF Jaguar had been shot down by a Sidewinder fired from an RAF Phantom in West Germany, turned out to be only too accurate.

During a station exercise at RAF Wildenrath in West Germany, Phantom aircraft of Nos 19 and 92 Squadrons were loaded with live weapons under simulated war conditions. This is a

Jaguar GR1 XX963 was the unwitting victim of a Sidewinder missile on 25 May 1982.
Crown Copyright

normal policy for exercising quick reaction alert (QRA) defence forces in NATO. For the purpose of the exercise other RAF Germany aircraft were treated as hostile forces. The aircrew briefing for those participating in the exercise covered safety precautions for the carriage of live weapons, which are intended to prevent the weapons being launched inadvertently.

On 25 May, a Phantom FG1 belonging to No 92 Squadron participating in the exercise took-off from RAF Wildenrath to mount a combat air patrol (CAP) under the control of a Sector Operations Centre (SOC). Shortly after take-off the crew ran through their pre-attack checks, which armed the air-to-air weapons – Sidewinder AIM-9s.

At this time the navigator, Flt Lt Alistair Invergarity – who was engaged in other tasks – did not monitor the pilot's actions and thus was unaware that the pilot, Flt Lt Roy Lawrence, had rendered live one of the two main safety switches.

Later in the sortie the Phantom's radar detected a contact which the pilot later identified as a pair of Jaguars. In accordance with the exercise scenario, the Phantom crew decided to engage. The crew then followed the normal procedures for a simulated attack and completed a typical engagement which culminated in the pilot pulling the weapon release trigger. When inert training weapons are carried this action simply produces a witness mark on the film record.

But in this case a Sidewinder missile was launched which struck one of the Jaguar aircraft.

Jaguar GR1, XX963 of No 14 Squadron based at RAF Bruggen, was being flown by Flt Lt Stephen Griggs as the No 2 of a pair of aircraft on a routine training sortie. The pilot detected an aircraft, which he thought was a Phantom, approaching the formation head-on and reported this to his leader. The indication disappeared and then reappeared from the rear. Shortly afterwards there was a loud explosion and the aircraft became uncontrollable. It had been struck by a Sidewinder.

The Jaguar leader saw the explosion and fire and called Flt Lt Griggs to eject, which he did. He landed in a field, sustaining only minor injuries, and was subsequently rescued by helicopter. The Jaguar crashed in open farmland and was destroyed.

The investigating Board of Inquiry established the cause of the accident was the inadvertent firing of the missile by the Phantom crew who, when airborne, followed the procedures applicable to an unarmed aircraft despite carrying live weapons. It was not established positively why the experienced and well qualified pilot forgot the real situation. However, it was found that the master armament switch in the pilot's cockpit had not been taped in the safe position, which it should have been. In addition, it was found that a circuit breaker in the rear cockpit – which was normally used to isolate the firing system – was unreliable in that it was possible to depress the circuit breaker stalk just sufficiently to make electrical contact and render the circuit live, but without pushing the circuit breaker fully home.

A further prescribed safety procedure not under the direct control of the crew also failed. The SOC are required to broadcast a 'check switches safe' call during any interception by an armed aircraft. In this case, however, there was a breakdown in communications caused by a simulated exercise emergency at RAF Wildenrath at the same time and the SOC, not having been told that the Phantom was armed, did not transmit the warning call.

Once again, this accident resulted from a combination of failures which together caused prescribed safety procedures to be disregarded or rendered ineffective. However, it was determined that the ultimate responsibility for the loss of Jaguar XX963 lay with the Phantom crew who were tried by Court Martial and found guilty of offences of negligence. Flt Lt Lawrence was found guilty of neglecting the use of an aircraft, and negligently causing the loss of an aircraft, while Flt Lt Invergarity was found guilty of negligently causing the loss of an aircraft and negligently allowing the loss of an aircraft. They were both sentenced to be severely reprimanded.

An immediate revision of regulations governing flights by armed aircraft in peacetime was set in hand and new orders were subsequently issued. A modification to provide a safety pin for the trigger rather than relying on a circuit-breaker was fitted to Phantom rear cockpits as an electrical isolation switch.

Although similar accidents have occurred in other services — a USAF B-52 on a training mission over New Mexico in 1961 was shot down by a Sidewinder accidentally fired from a F-100 — the accident of 25 May was thankfully the first and last such accident involving aircraft of the RAF.

Sidewinder air-to-air missiles being loaded on to RAF Phantom. *Duncan Cubitt*

Left:
Gazelle AH1 XX402 of 3CBAS shot down by Argentine small-arms fire on 21 May 1982. *Simon Falla*

Right:
Scout AH1 XT629 of 3CBAS shot down by an Argentine Pucara on 28 May 1982. *R. McLeod*

Date	Type	Serial	Sqn	Location	Remarks
25/05	Wessex HU5	XS512	848 Sqn	*Atlantic Conveyor*, South Atlantic	Lost during sinking of *Atlantic Conveyor* by Argentine Exocet missile
25/05	Wessex HU5	ST476	848 Sqn	*Atlantic Conveyor*, South Atlantic	Lost during sinking of *Atlantic Conveyor* by Argentine Exocet missile
25/05	Wessex HU5	XT483	848 Sqn	*Atlantic Conveyor*, South Atlantic	Lost during sinking of *Atlantic Conveyor* by Argentine Exocet missile
25/05	Chinook HC1	ZA706	18 Sqn	*Atlantic Conveyor*, South Atlantic	Lost during sinking of *Atlantic Conveyor* by Argentine Exocet missile
25/05	Chinook HC1	ZA716	18 Sqn	*Atlantic Conveyor*, South Atlantic	Lost during sinking of *Atlantic Conveyor* by Argentine Exocet missile
25/05	Chinook HC1	ZA719	18 Sqn	*Atlantic Conveyor*, South Atlantic	Lost during sinking of *Atlantic Conveyor* by Argentine Exocet missile
25/05	Lynx HAS2	XZ700	815 Sqn	*Atlantic Conveyor*, South Atlantic	Lost during sinking of *Atlantic Conveyor* by Argentine Exocet missile
25/05	Lynx HAS2	XZ242	815 Sqn	HMS *Coventry*, South Atlantic	Destroyed by Argentine bomb during sinking of *Coventry*
27/05	Harrier GR3	XZ988	1 Sqn	Goose Green, Falkland Is	Shot down by Argentine AA gunfire; Ej
28/05	Scout AH1	XT629	3CBAS	Nr Goose Green, Falkland Is	Shot down by Argentine Pucara; 1F
28/05	Sea Harrier FRS1	ZA174	801 Sqn	HMS *Invincible*, South Atlantic	Slid off deck while taxiing; Ej
30/05	Harrier GR3	XZ963	1 Sqn	Nr Stanley Airport, Falkland Is	Shot down by Argentine small-arms fire; Ej
01/06	Sea Harrier FRS1	XZ456	801 Sqn	Nr Stanley Airport, Falkland Is	Shot down by Argentine SAM; Ej
06/06	Gazelle AH1	XX377	3CBAS	Mt Pleasant, Falkland Is	Shot down by British SAM; 4F
08/06	Harrier GR3	XZ989	1 Sqn	Port San Carlos, Falkland Is	Emergency landing following loss of power
08/06	Harrier GR3	XV744	233 OCU	RAF Wittering	Crashed on landing following loss of power
11/06	Jaguar GR1	XX820	31 Sqn	RAF Bruggen, WG	Abandoned following engine explosion after overshoot; Ej
11/06	Gazelle AH1	XW896	BATUS	Suffield Range, Canada	Crashed into high ground during low flying flight
12/06	Wessex HAS3	XM837	737 Sqn	HMS *Glamorgan*, South Atlantic	Destroyed aboard *Glamorgan* by land-fired Argentine Exocet
17/06	Buccaneer S2B	XX898	12 Sqn	Nr Lossiemouth	Abandoned following loss of control on approach; Ej

18 May 1982: Sea King HC4 ZA290

A total of five Royal Navy Sea King helicopters were lost in the South Atlantic during the Falklands conflict: four of them were due to accidents – but one was not.

Having embarked on HMS *Hermes* at Portsmouth on 5 April 1982, Sea King HC4 ZA290, a navalised version of the Commando assault helicopter belonging to 846 NAS, sailed with the carrier bound for the South Atlantic. On 1 May, *Hermes* entered the TEZ and 16 days later ZA290 transferred to HMS *Invincible* along with its sister aircraft ZA292 which was to act as reserve machine. On the evening of 17 May, the carrier launched the Sea King while making a high-speed dash well to the west of the Falklands. The crew of ZA290 comprised Lt Richard Hutchings RM, pilot; Lt Alan Bennett RN, co-pilot; and LACMN Imrie (aircrewman).

The following evening it was announced in London that Sea King ZA290 which, according to the MoD, 'had been on anti-submarine operations from a Task Force ship and had lost its way', and later 'to have force-landed in Chile as a result of engine failure due to weather conditions'.

However, when the burnt-out remains of the Sea King were accidentally discovered on a remote beach at Agua Fresca close to Dawson Island, a government prison camp some 11 miles south of Punta Arenas in Chile, a different story of the helicopter's one-way mission soon emerged.

It had reportedly taken-off with a contingent of SAS and flown to the South American mainland on a covert mission – 'to land the troops near one or more of the Argentinian air bases, to report by radio when aircraft were taking off and assembling to launch attacks'. After disembarking the SAS teams, the Sea King landed on the beach at Agua Fresca where it was burnt by its crew, They were then picked up by a Chilean Air Force helicopter and taken to Punta Arenas where they officially gave themselves up to the Chilean authorities a few days later. They later returned to the UK via Santiago.

Following the press discovery, the British helicopter's remains were buried by the Chileans on site. It was also alleged that a number of aircraft had been destroyed on the ground at the Argentine Navy's Rio Grande base – located only 25 miles from the Chilean border – a few days after the Sea King left the carrier. But this report, or the real mission of ZA290, was never confirmed by the MoD despite the award of the DSC to Lts Hutchings and Bennett, and the DFM to LACMN Imrie, which was unlikely to have been awarded to a crew for allegedly losing their way and their aircraft.

Sea King HC4 ZA290 lost its way in Chile.
Royal Navy

4 May 1982: Sea Harrier FRS1 XZ450

On 5 April 1982, 800 Naval Air Squadron (NAS) sailed from Portsmouth for the South Atlantic aboard the British Task Force carrier HMS *Hermes* which entered the Falkland Islands Total Exclusion Zone (TEZ) on 1 May. On that day the squadron's Sea Harrier FRS1s carried out their first raid against Argentine forces at Stanley Airport and Goose Green without loss.

On the afternoon of 4 May, a second attack on Goose Green was launched from *Hermes*. Two of the three Sea Harriers, flown by the Flight Leader Lt-Cdr Batt and Lt Nick Taylor, were armed with three CBUs (Cluster Bomb Unit), while the third flown by Flt Lt Ted Ball, an RAF exchange officer, carried three 1,000lb retard bombs. Nick Taylor, flying Sea Harrier XZ450 — the first production FRS1 and an ex-MoD(PE) Sea Eagle ASM development aircraft — followed 'Gordy' Batt in a fast low-level run-in on the strip from the southeast. At the same time, Ted Ball lined up for a run-in from the southwest and was in a position to witness the loss of XZ450.

'I had approached the target at high level before dropping to 80ft for the final run-in. We planned that I should arrive over the target slightly after Nick so that I would miss the blast from his 1,000-pounder. As I began my run-in at 500kt and as low as possible, I kept a watch out for where I knew Nick would be coming in. Almost as soon as I spotted him I saw a small explosion which was followed by a larger one, then his aircraft hit the ground and disintegrated in a ball of fire in front of me. By the time I had taken my eyes off Nick's aircraft, I was almost over my target and had to make some rapid adjustments in order to hit it. Most of the fire was now aimed at me but although it must have been pretty heavy, I was completely unaware of it at the time.'

Flt Lt Ball subsequently joined up with Lt-Cdr Batt and both aircraft made a safe recovery to *Hermes* only 50min after launching.

The remains of XZ450, thought to have been shot down by a 35mm Oerlikon gun, came to rest in a field adjacent to the eastern perimeter of Goose Green airstrip. Lt Nick Taylor was killed outright, the first British pilot to lose his life in the Falklands conflict, and the first to fall to enemy fire since the Suez campaign more than a quarter-of-a-century earlier.

As a result of this loss, low-level bombing was considered an unacceptable risk and whenever possible, toss-bombing became the normal method of attack against ground targets. However, the Section Leader on that fateful second Goose Green attack, Lt-Cdr Gordon Batt, was to lose his life on 24 May when his Sea Harrier crashed into the sea some 90 miles northeast of Port Stanley shortly after taking off from HMS *Hermes* for a night raid on Stanley Airport.

For the duration of the South Atlantic conflict, normal peacetime accident investigation procedures were not followed. There was no time to convene Boards of Inquiry in the heat of battle and it was some months — and in a few cases, years — before the full facts of British aircraft losses in the Falklands were officially released.

Victor K2 XL232, 15 October 1982.

Date	Type	Serial	Unit	Location	Remarks
29/06	Harrier T4A	XW272	4 Sqn	Hohne Range, WG	Crashed on take-off from grass; 1F
07/07	Phantom FGR2	XV272	29 Sqn	Nr Cromer	Flew into sea in fog; 2F
11/07	Sea King HAS2	XV698	–	Channel	Ditched in sea following engine failure in 70ft hover
28/07	Hawk T1	XX305	4FTS	RAF Valley	Stalled during emergency landing, Ej; 1F
05/08	Hunter T7	XL593	1TWU	5nm NE Carmarthen	Abandoned following engine failure; Ej
24/08	Gazelle AH1	XX452	–	Middle Wallop	Incorrect control input
13/09	Jaguar GR1	XX760	14 Sqn	Nr Brora, WG	Abandoned following engine fire: Ej
15/09	Gazelle AH1	XX373	663 Sqn	WG	Tail rotor stall
20/09	Buccaneer S2B	XV160	16 Sqn	Capo Frasca Range, Sardinia	Abandoned following structural failure during spin; Ej
21/09	Lynx HAS2	XZ256	815 Sqn	–	Tail rotor struck by wave during engine run-up on deck; DBR
28/09	Scout AH1	–	A&AEE	Boscombe Down	–
29/09	Jaguar GR1	XX768	17 Sqn	Nr Heinsberg-Randerath	Abandoned following engine fire; Ej
30/09	Lynx HAS2	XZ247	815 Sqn	South Atlantic	Ditched in sea following in-flight fire
15/10	Victor K2	XL232	55 Sqn	RAF Marham	Engine explosion and fire on take-off
20/10	Hawk T1	XX300	2TWU	RAF Chivenor	Abandoned following birdstrike at night on finals; Ej
28/10	Wasp HAS1	XS568	–	–	Ditched in sea following loss of power in hover
06/11	Harrier GR3	XW767	–	RAF Stanley, Falkland Is	Crashed into sea following engine failure; Ej
01/12	Gazelle AH1	XX400	AAC	NI	Crashed following wirestrike
09/12	Jet Provost T5A	XW417	7FTS	Lake Thirlmere, Cumbria	Flew into high ground in bad weather; 1F
16/12	Hunter GA11	WT702	FRADU	Channel	Crashed into sea during low pass; 1F

1983

Date	Type	Serial	Unit	Location	Cause
21/01	Sea Harrier FRS1	ZA177	899 Sqn	Cattistock	Abandoned following failure to recover from inverted spin; Ej
01/02	Beaver AL1	XV272	AAC	Nr Popham, Hants	Heavy landing during field exercise
03/02	Sea King HAS5	XV658	820 Sqn	HMS *Invincible*, Portugal	Ditched in sea following loss of tail rotor; 1F
23/02	Harrier GR3	XV795	233 OCU	Nr Peterborough	Mid-air collision; Ej
23/02	Harrier T4	XW926	233 OCU	Nr Peterborough	Mid-air collision; 2F
07/03	Jaguar GR1	XZ376	17 Sqn	Nr Tain Range, Scotland	Abandoned following engine failure; Ej
22/03	Harrier GR3	XV787	1453 Flt	Nr RAF Stanley, Falkland Is	Crashed into sea following engine failure; Ej
30/03	Jet Provost T3A	XN495	7FTS	Elvington	Bellylanding following engine failure
16/04	Cadet TX3	–	614GS	Nr Wethersfield	Broke-up during aerobatics; 2F
19/04	Jaguar GR1	XX742	6 Sqn	North Sea off Norfolk coast	Abandoned following loss of control; Ej
20/04	Gazelle HT3	XX374	2FTS	Mt Snowdon	Crashed during unauthorised low-level flight; 2F
21/04	Hawk T1	XX227	CFS	Nr Culachy, Scotland	Wirestrike at low-level (Red Arrows); Backseat Ej
26/04	Hawk T1	–	4FTS	North Sea	Backseat Ej
03/05	Harrier GR3	XZ134	–	Lippstadt, WG	Abandoned on take-off following engine failure; Ej
04/05	Lynx HAS2	XZ249	815 Sqn	Gulf of Oman	Ditched in sea following loss of tail rotor control
16/05	Hunter GA11	XE716	FRADU	English Channel	Abandoned following engine failure; Ej
27/05	Wasp HAS1	XV638	829 Sqn	South Atlantic	Ditched in sea following engine surge
06/06	Wasp HAS1	XT782	–	–	Heavy landing following 'top hat' section lifting; DBR
11/06	Alouette AH2	XR380	UNFIYCYP	Cyprus	Underslung load caught on skid, aircraft rolled down hillside
14/06	Sea Harrier FRS1	XZ500	800 Sqn	HMS *Illustrious*, Bay of Biscay	Abandoned over sea following loss of control during test flight; Ej
16/06	Jaguar GR1	XZ105	2 Sqn	Nr Goose Bay, Canada	Mid-air collision; Ej
16/06	Jaguar GR1	XZ110	2 Sqn	Nr Goose Bay, Canada	Mid-air collision; Ej
22/06	Jaguar GR1	XX721	54 Sqn	Nr Hahn, WG	Abandoned following fuel starvation on take-off (Danish pilot); Ej
24/06	Hawk T1	XX721	4FTS	Isle of Man	Crashed into high ground; 2F
06/07	Wasp HAS1	XT795	–	–	Crashed during landing on rolling ship

20 April 1983: Gazelle HT3 XX374

Circumstances:
On the morning of 20 April 1983, Gazelle XX374 was being flown on a dual sortie comprising a medium and low-level navigation exercise from RAF Shawbury to Snowdonia, followed by instruction in mountain flying. The crew for this sortie consisted of an RAF Qualified Helicopter Instructor (QHI) and a Brunei student who was preparing for the start of a helicopter instructor course.

The transit to the mountain area was completed uneventfully in clear, calm weather, and the pilot made several routine calls reporting his position in Snowdonia and advising that the flight was proceeding normally. During this time the aircraft was seen in the vicinity of two trains on the Snowdon Mountain Railway before it circled the summit of Snowdon. The aircraft then departed the summit in an easterly direction and descended into Cwn Dyli where it turned and hover-taxied alongside the miner's track. During this slow flight, which was carried out level with the track – but displaced a few yards to one side – the student instructor waved at observers on the ground.

The aircraft, with the RAF QHI in control, then came to a hover just in front of a party of school children and their teachers. It remained in this position for some 10-15sec before it turned and accelerated away in a descent over Llyn Teryn. When approximately ¼ mile away, eyewitnesses saw the aircraft pull up into an ever-steepening climb, almost reaching the vertical, before it executed a wing-over to reverse the direction of flight. On completion of this manoeuvre, the aircraft rejoined the miner's track and flew towards the school party at high speed in a gently descending turn. The aircraft passed very low over the party then, when some 70ft beyond them, part of the aircraft hit the ground. Control of the aircraft was lost and it proceeded to bounce along the track on its side before it left the track and fell down the valley slope. It eventually disintegrated when it collided with a large boulder. Assistance was quickly to hand but both crew members had suffered fatal injuries. There was no fire in the wreckage or other casualties.

Cause:
Eyewitness evidence as to the manoeuvres flown immediately prior to the accident, and subsequent examination of the wreckage, suggested that the aircraft itself was serviceable and performing normally up to the time of impact. It was concluded that the RAF instructor had carried out an impromptu and unauthorised low flypast for the benefit of the school party on the track and, probably because of an optical illusion caused by a spur of rock just beyond the party position, had misjudged his recovery to the extent that the aircraft struck the ground.

Gazelle — the photograph shows an Army AH1.

Harrier GR3 XV795 and Harrier T4 XW926 collided in mid-air over Cambridgeshire, 23 February 1983.
Peterborough Evening Telegraph via A. Goodrum

27 July 1983: Beaver AL1 XP811

Circumstances:

The pilot of an Army Air Corps Beaver was tasked as part of the air display for the RNAS Culdrose Air Day to give a single aircraft display to show the capabilities of the Beaver aircraft. The Army Beaver is a light single-engined six-seat liaison aircraft capable of operating from field airstrips, and the Army has a total of nine such aircraft deployed mainly in Northern Ireland and at Middle Wallop. The pilot, a retired AAC officer employed as a civilian instructor, flew the aircraft from Middle Wallop to Culdrose during the morning of 27 July and attended a display briefing there at 11.00hrs. He took off at 15.30hrs for his part in the display. He climbed to 100ft before his normal display sequence which was to start with a figure-eight manoeuvre in front of the crowd line. It was during the second 360° turn to the left that the port wing of the aircraft struck the ground and the aircraft crashed clear of the crowd on the airfield 2min after take-off. All emergency services were on the scene within 60sec. There was no fire but the pilot was confirmed dead shortly after he was pulled clear of the wreckage.

Cause:

The investigation found that the existing meteorological conditions were a major factor in the cause of the accident. At the time of the crash, the wind was gusting up to 27kt at right angles to the centre of the display axis which itself was parallel with the crowd line. This caused the aircraft to be blown towards the crowd line. As the pilot was approaching his second turn he was flying a gradual slope, which may not have been apparent to him. The combination of wind and slope could possibly have given the pilot an impression of considerable speed over the ground when approaching the crowd line. He may have then reduced his airspeed to a state where his safety margin above stalling speed was slight. All other possible causes were studied, including technical failure, but expert investigation of the weckage found no evidence of any technical defect. The pilot was a very experienced instructor with over 6,000 flying hours, and the display which he had performed on previous occasions was within his capabilities.

AAC Beaver AL1. *Duncan Cubitt*

96

Hawker Sidd XV742 crashed on Holbeach Range,
28 October 1983.
Lincolnshire Free Press via A. Goodrum

17 Oct 1983: Phantom FGR2 XV484

Circumstances:

XV484 based at RAF Stanley in the Falklands, was acting as a simulated target for a pair of Phantoms which were mounting a Combat Air Patrol (CAP) during a routine training sortie. The pair had taken off first in order to fly a short navigation exercise prior to the CAP at medium altitude. The weather was generally good, with excellent visibility below broken medium level cloud over the exercise area, which was part of the flat low-lying southern area of East Falkland. To the north of this, however, high ground was covered by more extensive cloud, with bases down to a height of 1,500ft above sea level.

A successful simulated engagement between the three aircraft took place towards the eastern end of the exercise area and at its conclusion XV484 was seen to depart on a westerly heading, below cloud, and at a height of about 1,000ft, in order to position for a further run through the exercise area as a target.

The pair of Phantoms resumed their CAP and shortly afterwards one of their radars detected a contact. However, this faded from the radar display within a few seconds. Subsequently, black smoke was seen above the cloud to the northwest of the pair. At the time this was attributed to a peat fire, but after several minutes had elapsed and no radar or radio contact with XV484 had been established, the appearance of the smoke assumed a greater significance. Search and Rescue operations were mounted and the wreckage of XV484 was found. The aircraft had hit the cloud-covered slope of Mount Usborne 2 some 500ft below the summit of the ridge which rises to 2,300ft. The aircraft disintegrated on

impact and the crew, neither of which had initiated ejection, had been killed.

Cause:

A painstaking investigation found no evidence of technical failure. It was also possible to rule out all likely external hazards which could have contributed to the accident. Ostensibly, XV484 had been operating normally and was in controlled flight when the aircraft hit the ground. It was therefore concluded that the crew may have been making a

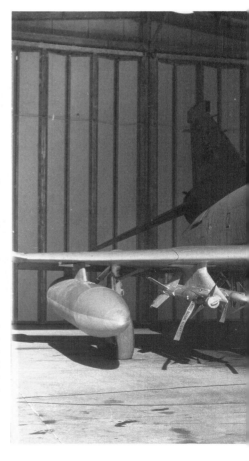

Phantom FGR2 in the Falklands.

98

deliberate descent through cloud unaware of their actual position relative to the high ground. Some corroboration of this theory was subsequently obtained from specialist evidence which revealed that at impact, the aircraft's inertially derived present position display was indicating a position some 8½nm southwest of the crash site. This indication would have suggested to the crew that they were over the low ground vicinity of Goose Green. Nevertheless, in accordance with standard operating procedures (SOP), the crew should not have relied solely and implicitly on the aircraft's intertial navigation system to fix their position before descending through cloud. Consequently, the erroneous present position indication could not be regarded in isolation as being a major contributory cause of this tragic accident. Indeed, because of the limited and largely circumstantial evidence available, the precise cause will never be known.

08/07	Hawk T1	XX195	2TWU	Nr Dyfed, Wales	Emergency landing following wirestrike; DBR
27/07	Beaver AL1	XP811	AAC	RNAS Culdrose	Stalled at low-level during aerobatic display; 1F
29/07	Hawk T1	XX229	1TWU	Irish Sea	Abandoned over sea following low-level flame-out; Ej
29/07	Hawk T1	XX336	2TWU	Bristol Channel	Abandoned over sea following mid-air collision; Ej
29/07	Hawk T1	XX353	2TWU	Bristol Channel	Abandoned over sea; Ej
03/08	Canberra T17	WJ625	360 Sqn	Gibraltar	Crashed into sea after take-off following loss of control; 3F
11/08	Buccaneer S2B	XX891	16 Sqn	RAF Laarbruch, WG	Stalled on approach; 1F
26/08	Lightning F3	XP753	LTF	Nr Scarborough	Crashed into sea during low-level aerobatics; 1F
06/09	Wasp HAS1	XT427	–	–	Ditched in sea following loss of power during take-off
19/09	Jaguar GR1	XX114	226 OCU	RAF Lossiemouth	Abandoned following birdstrike; Ej
27/09	Tornado GR1	ZA586	9 Sqn	Nr King's Lynn	Abandoned following loss of power (first loss of Tornado); Ej; 1F (Sqn Ldr Michael Stephens – Pilot)
29/09	Gazelle AH1	XX376	3CBAS	Soest, WG	Heavy emergency landing

Canberra T17 WJ625 of No 360 Squadron which crashed into the sea on 3 August 1983.

Date	Type	Serial	Unit	Location	Cause
14/10	Chipmunk T10	WK613	BFWF	Middle Wallop	Hit obstacle during landing
17/10	Phantom FGR2	XV484	23 Sqn	East Falklands	Crashed into mountain in cloud; 2F
20/10	Sea Harrier FRS1	ZA194	899 Sqn	Nr Dorchester	Abandoned following control restriction (USMC pilot); Ej
24/10	Gazelle AH1	XX313	AAC	Barton Stacey, Hants	Incorrect control input during training flight
28/10	Tornado GR1	ZA558	617 Sqn	Nr Sherington, Norfolk	Flew into sea, 1F
28/10	Harrier GR3	XV742	233 OCU	Holbeach Range	Flew into sea following hit by ricochet while firing on range; 1F
14/11	Tornado GR1	ZA597	9 Sqn	RAF Honington	Heavy landing, DBR
19/11	Harrier GR3	XV762	1453 Flt	Nr Goose Green, Falkland Is	Crashed into high ground; 1F
21/11	Jet Provost T3	XM453	3FTS	Nr Ingleton, Yorks	Abandoned following birdstrike; Ej
07/12	Wessex HU5	–	–	Setermoen, Norway	Whiteout on take-off; 4I

1984

Date	Type	Serial	Unit	Location	Cause
05/01	Lynx AH1	XZ681	AAC	West Falklands	Crashed into sea; 2F
17/01	Jaguar T2	XX915	ETPS	Nr Porton Down, Wilts	Abandoned on approach to Boscombe Down; Ej; 1F
06/02	Tornado GR1	ZA451	15 Sqn	Nr Jever, WG	Abandoned following lightning strike; Ej
07/02	Jaguar GR1	XX750	6/14 Sqn	90nm NW Nellis Range, USA	Flew into ground during low-level flight (Red Flag); 1F
07/02	Hawk T1	XX288	2TWU	Swansea Airport	Abandoned after touchdown following engine malfunction; Ej
29/02	Sea King HC4	ZA297	–	Bardufoss, Norway	Hit electricity cables
05/03	Phantom FGR2	XT891	228 OCU	RAF Waddington	Abandoned on overshoot; Ej
16/03	Sea Harrier FRS1	XZ496	800 Sqn	HMS *Illustrious*, Norway	Abandoned over sea following total loss of power on finals; Ej
21/03	Hawk T1	XX251	CFS	RAF Akrotiri, Cyprus	Abandoned after striking ground during practice 'opposition loop' (Red Arrows); Ej
13/04	Wasp HAS1	XT794	829 Sqn	Ascension Is	Ditched in sea following power loss on lift-off

Tornado GR1 ZA494, 18 July 1984.
Crown Copyright.

8 Nov 1984: Tornado GR1 ZA603

Circumstances:
Tornado ZA603 was detached to RAF Laarbruch in West Germany when, on 8 November 1984, it took off as the lead aircraft of a pair for a low-level training sortie in southern Germany. The sortie proceeded normally until the two aircraft were travelling towards the second target when the pilot saw a USAF A-10 aircraft on a collision course immediately ahead of his aircraft. He pulled up suddenly and banked the aircraft to the left to avoid the A-10. The navigator, who had been looking down into the cockpit to study the Projected Map Display, was forced down by the acceleration ('g' force) into an unfamiliar position. He looked out to the left and saw the ground but no horizon. Sensing that the aircraft was rolling rapidly to the left and descending, and believing the aircraft to be out of control and about to crash, he ejected. Tornado ZA603 had the facility for command ejection selected to 'Both'. As a result, the pilot was automatically ejected as soon as the navigator had left the aircraft. The aircraft crashed in open country and was destroyed.

Cause:
Examination of the Accident Data Recorder (ADR) read-out revealed that the aircraft had been serviceable up to the moment when the crew ejected. It became apparent that the navigator's head-down posture at the beginning of the evasive manoeuvre, and the force to which he had been subjected, had resulted in him becoming disorientated to such an extent that he thought the aircraft was rolling rapidly to the left and descending. As a result, he had considered that the aircraft was about to crash and so had seen his only option as ejection. Appropriate action has been taken.

Subsequent actions:
New procedures for the setting of the Command Ejection Lever in Tornados have been introduced.

Tornado GR1.

11/05	Jet Provost T3		1FTS	RAF Linton-on-Ouse	Hit barrier on landing; DBR
20/05	Buccaneer S2B	XZ430	208 Sqn	Moray Firth, Scotland	Flew into sea on low-level exercise; 2F
03/06	Nimrod MR2	XV257	42 Sqn	Nr Land's End	Emergency landing following flare fire in bomb bay after take-off
03/06	Harrier GR3	XZ135	4 Sqn	Aschaffenburg, WG	Abandoned after emergency landing during air display following engine fire; Ej; 1F (Ground)
22/06	Gazelle AH1	XZ770	BATUS	Nr Alberta, Canada	Crashed into ground during night exercise (Medicine Hat); 1F
12/07	Tornado GR1	ZA408	TWCU	Nr Sherrington, Norfolk	Abandoned following mid-air collision; Ej
12/07	Jaguar GR1	XZ393	54 Sqn	Nr Sherrington, Norfolk	Crashed into sea following mid-air collision; Ej
13/07	Lightning F6	XS920	5 Sqn	Nr Henslingen, WG	Crashed into ground following wirestrike during combat practice with A-10A; 1F
18/07	Tornado GR1	ZA494	27 Sqn	Goose Bay, Canada	Abandoned following loss of control on finals; Ej
27/07	Hunter T7	–	RAE	RAE Bedford	Bellylanding; DBR
15/08	Jet Provost T3	XN473	7FTS	RAF Cranwell	Crashed after take-off following birdstrike; DBR

Jaguar T2 XX915 of the ETPS which was abandoned on approach to Boscombe Down, 17 January 1984. *Air Britain*

Argosy C1 XN817, 1 October 1984.
Crown Copyright

22/08	Jaguar GR1	XZ395	54 Sqn	20nm E of Cromer	Crashed into sea following loss of control; Ej
30/08	Sea King HAS5	XV665	810 Sqn	RNAS Culdrose	Rolled over on landing
31/08	Hawk T1	XX257	CFS	Nr Sidmouth, Devon	Abandoned following engine failure during low-level display (Red Arrows); Ej
26/09	Sea King HAS5	ZA134	820 Sqn	English Channel	Ditched in sea following failure of engine in hover
01/10	Argosy C1	XN817	AAEE	West Freugh, Scotland	Heavy landing; DBR
25/10	Hawk T1	XX298	4FTS	Tremadoc Bay, Wales	Abandoned following loss of control; Ej
31/10	Hunter T8C	XL584	FRADU	Nr Isle of Wight	Crashed into sea during low level sortie; 1F
07/11	Hawk T1	XX180	4FTS	RAF Mona, Anglesey	Abandoned in circuit following birdstrike; Ej
08/11	Tornado GR1	ZA603	27 Sqn	Nr Schweinfurt, WG	Crashed following accidental ejection by navigator; Ej
08/11	Lightning F6	XR761	5 Sqn	21nm NE Binbrook	Abandoned over sea following engine fire; Ej
14/11	Chinook HC1	ZA676	240 OCU	Nr Basingstoke	Emergency landing following engine failure on take-off; DBR
29/11	Harrier GR3	XZ992	1453 Flt	RAF Stanley, Falkland Is	Abandoned over sea following birdstrike; Ej
01/12	Sea Harrier FRS1	XZ458	800 Sqn	HMS *Illustrious*, off Ft William	Abandoned following birdstrike during low level sortie; Ej
03/12	Wessex HU5	XT767	772 Sqn	Nr Portland	Hit harbour wall following control malfunction; 1F

Chinook HC1 ZA676, 14 November 1984.
Crown Copyright.

Date	Type	Serial	Unit	Location	Cause
24/01	Lynx AH1	XZ761	AAC	Bavaria, WG	Hit ski hut while landing during whiteout
30/01	Hawk T1	XX279	2TWU	Bristol Channel	Abandoned over sea following loss of control; Ej; 1F
07/02	Harrier T4N	ZB606	899 Sqn	RNAS Yeovilton	Crashed on to road following loss of control; 2F
15/02	Lynx HAS2	–	HMS *Brazen*	Falkland Is	Ditched in sea
18/02	Harrier T4	XW933	3 Sqn	Nr Gutersloh, WG	Abandoned following mid-air collision with *Kriegsmarine* F-104; 1F
05/03	Wasp HAS1	XT423	HMS *Endurance*	Port Stanley, Falkland Is	Ditched at sea following engine failure
06/03	Lightning F6	XR772	5 Sqn	Nr Spurn Point	Abandoned over sea following loss of control; Ej; 1F
12/03	Scout AH1	XW906	660 Sqn	Crest Hill CP, HK	Rolled over on take-off following loss of rotor speed; 1F
25/03	Bulldog T1	XX660	Oxford UAS	Nr Yeldon, Oxon	Abandoned following loss of control during spin; 1F
01/04	Jaguar GR1	XZ388	14 Sqn	Nr Hapsburg, WG	Abandoned following loss of control at low-level due to head-down radio frequency change; Ej
17/04	Hawk T1	XX293	4FTS	RAF Wattisham	Abandoned following loss of control on take-off due to canopy coming off; Ej
17/04	Sea Fury T20	VZ345	A&AEE	Boscombe Down	Ground loop after landing; DBR
14/06	Buccaneer S2B	XV341	12 Sqn	RAF Lossiemouth	Abandoned following loss of control due to tailplane linkage failure on finals; Ej; 1F
21/06	Sea King HC4	ZD635	810 Sqn	Nr Dundee	Crashed into hillside with underslung load having run out of fuel; 1F
27/06	Sea King HAS5	XZ919	810 Sqn	Falkland Is	Mid-air collision with RAF Hercules; 4F
09/07	Jaguar GR1A	XZ365	2 Sqn	Nr Mohne-See, WG	Abandoned following striking high ground in bad weather; Ej
08/08	Canberra B2	WK162	100 Sqn	RAF Alconbury	Aborted take-off following ASI failure; DBR
18/09	Scout AH1	–	–	Wroughton	Forced landing
19/09	Lightning F6	XS921	11 Sqn	50nm NE Withamsea	Abandoned over sea following control failure; Ej
26/09	Hawk T1	XX333	2 TWU	Deccimomannu Range, Sardinia	Abandoned over sea following mid-air collision; Ej

Jaguar Mid-Air Collisions

On 8 September 1910, two aeroplanes piloted by brothers named Warcha-lovski collided in mid-air at Wiener-Neustadt, Austria, the world's first recorded air collision. The only injury on that occasion was a broken leg. Since those pioneering days of flight, and as the sky became increasingly crowded, the mid-air collision has become an increasingly common hazard for all pilots, and military pilots in particular. While all Service pilots have the benefit of being trained to fly in close formation, many collisions occur during routine training flights, occasionally during tail chases, or over ranges when the pilot, especially the fast jet pilot, is momentarily distracted while trying to visually identify a target.

One of the commonest causes of the mid-air collision, however, is with high-speed aircraft manoeuvring in close formation, often at very low levels — where there is no margin for error. The following chapter deals with four mid-air collisions between similar types of aircraft, all of which occurred in similar circumstances.

On 10 December 1979 a formation of four Jaguar GR1s of No 226 OCU from RAF Lossiemouth, Morayshire, were flying near the village of Lumsden, Aberdeenshire, on a routine training flight when the accident occurred. The purpose of the training sortie was to give two student pilots practice of various types of formation flying under the supervision of two instructor pilots.

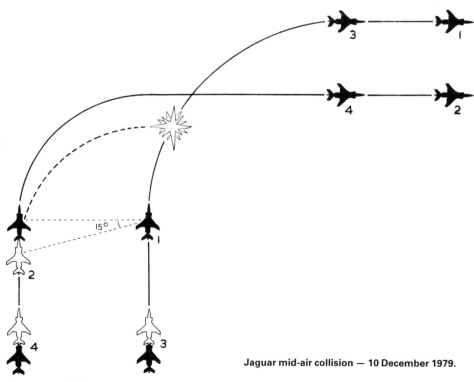

Jaguar mid-air collision — 10 December 1979.

108

The student involved in the accident was flying XX749 in the No 2 position, and although new to the Jaguar he was an experienced fast jet pilot. The pilot of the other aircraft involved, XX755, was one of the instructors, an experienced Jaguar pilot, who flew as No 3.

The weather was good throughout the flight and the four Jaguars practised manoeuvring in different formations before forming into 'Card'. Flying at a height of between 500ft and 1,000ft AGL (above ground level), the formation made several 90° turns in Card without incident. In order to maintain Card formation the line-abreast aircraft had to change stations from left to right or vice versa during a routine 90° turn.

The leader called for a 90° turn to the right, saw No 2 commence turning and, at the right moment, started his own turn, losing sight of No 2 as the latter passed behind him. The leader continued turning, expecting his No 2 to appear behind him and to the right, but instead saw a fireball. Nos 2 and 3 had collided. No 2, the student pilot, ejected but suffered serious injury, while No 3, the instructor, failed to eject and was killed. Both aircraft were destroyed.

Although No 2 may have been slightly behind the leader, instead of parallel and at the same height — thus above Nos 3 and 4 during the crossover — the only possible reason for the collision was that No 2 had failed to keep an adequate lookout for No 3.

Less than a year later, a similar collision between Jaguars occurred over Germany. On 28 May 1980, a formation of four Jaguar GR1s belonging to No 17 Squadron were in 'Arrow' formation flying at 420kt at 500ft returning to their base at RAF Bruggen for a standard break and landing in good weather. The two aircraft involved in the collision were Nos 1 and 2, XX961 and XX964,

both flown by experienced Jaguar pilots. After pulling to 1,000ft over the base, the leader broke normally and once established in his turn on to a downwind leg, looked back and saw that No 2 aircraft was very close to him and getting closer. Realising that a collision was imminent, the leader attempted to change his flightpath but there was insufficient time for his aircraft to react. The two Jaguars collided and caught fire.

The leader ejected and was uninjured but the No 2 failed to eject and was killed. No evidence of technical malfunction of either aircraft, both of which were destroyed in the crash, was found by the Board of Inquiry.

As with the previous accident, it was possible that No 2 had, for some reason lost sight of the leader and did not remain level for the standard 2-3sec after the 'break' was called by the leader before commencing his turn. However he should have been below the leader's flightpath unless the leader had been slow in pulling up before making his turn.

Another mid-air collision between Jaguars occurred on 16 June 1983 at Goose Bay during a regular squadron deployment to Canada for the purposes of tactical training.

A three-Jaguar formation flown by experienced pilots from No 2 Squadron based at RAF Laarbruch in West Germany, was recovering to Goose Bay airfield for a visual join into the circuit. The circuit direction of the runway in use was specified as left hand, and the formation leader had pre-briefed that the join would be accomplished by the aircraft moving from tactical formation into close echelon starboard for a left-hand break. However, on contacting Air Traffic Control, the formation was instructed to fly a right-hand circuit, so

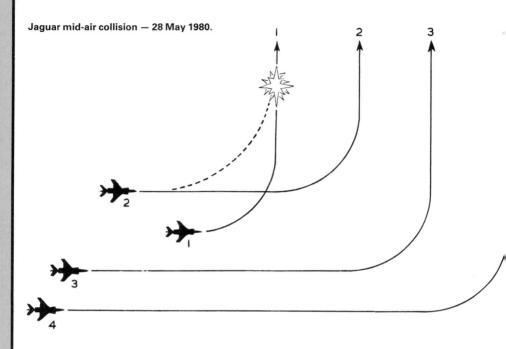

Jaguar mid-air collision — 28 May 1980.

the leader ordered his section to move from tactical formation into close echelon port. During the formation change Nos 2 and 3 aircraft, XZ105 and XZ110, collided. Both aircraft caught fire and the pilots ejected without injury. The aircraft crashed into water surrounding the airfield and were destroyed.

As the primary cause of the accident the Board of Inquiry determined that the pilot of No 3 aircraft had lost sight of No 2 while they were moving from tactical formation into close echelon port. When this occurred, he should have discontinued his movements and pulled up and out of the formation in order to re-establish visual contact with the No 2, whom it was his responsibility to avoid. He did not do so and a collision resulted.

The fourth mid-air collision involving

Jaguars in recent years occurred on 7 October 1985. Three Jaguar GR1s of No 6 Squadron from RAF Coltishall were flying a low-level sortie consisting of attacks on Holbeach and Cowden Ranges, followed by low-level tactical flying training. The weather was suitable for the sortie which had progressed as planned. The formation was west of the Pennine Ridge heading northwest with the No 2 aircraft, XX731, on the starboard side, closer than usual and slightly behind his leader, flying XX728. In an effort to regain line-abreast formation, the No 2 increased speed to 470-480kt. The leader commenced a starboard turn, which involved crossing over his No 2 at a pre-planned point. The No 2, who was still lagging behind the leader, whilst waiting for the leader to cross over, descended slightly to get some vertical separation before starting a gentle turn to starboard. The leader flew a slacker than normal turn, but once he had crossed, the No 2 tightened his own turn, climbing slightly to maintain height above the gently rising ground. After a brief check of his heading in a head-up display, the No 2 looked in his one o'clock position for the other aircraft, but was surprised to see it closer than expected in his two o'clock position. Realising that a collision was imminent he rolled his Jaguar and pushed the nose down to avoid the other aircraft, but immediately felt an impact and the cockpit filled with flames.

The No 2 tried to eject but missed the handle on the first attempt because his view was obscured by flames. His second attempt was successful although by this time he was at a dangerously low level. The pilot of the other aircraft must have been incapacitated in the collision for he was killed when his aircraft crashed, without attempting to eject.

The cause of the accident was again the No 2 pilot's failure to maintain an adequate lookout for his leader during the crossover turn, combined with the leader flying a slacker turn than expected.

Every one of these four accidents had a number of common features, apart from involving the same type of aircraft. All occurred while flying in close formation, at low level and high speed, and all involved the No 2 aircraft during crossover turns.

Although actions taken following all four accidents included the amending of RAF manuals to highlight the risk of collision during crossover turns, they are still considered as a 'standard manoeuvre' for fast-jet pilots. The cause for all four accidents was attributed to Aircrew Error (AE).

XX728 and XX731 collided on 7 October 1985. *MAP*

Lynx AH1 XZ761, 24 January 1985.

Date	Type	Serial	Unit	Location	Cause
26/09	Hawk T1	XX340	2 TWU	Deccimomannu Range, Sardinia	Abandoned over sea following mid-air collision; Ej
07/10	Jaguar GR1A	XX728	6 Sqn	Nr Alston, Cumbria	Abandoned following mid-air collision; Ej
07/10	Jaguar GR1A	XX731	6 Sqn	Nr Alston, Cumbria	Abandoned following mid-air collision; 1F
14/10	Sea King AEW2	–	849 Sqn	HMS *Invincible*, off Portugal	Ditched in sea
25/10	Wessex HC2	XT669	72 Sqn	Forkhill, Co Armagh	Hit radio mast during take-off; 1F
08/11	Sea King HAS5	XZ918	814 Sqn	Mediterranean	Ditched in sea following loss of main gearbox oil
19/11	Harrier GR3	XW922	–	RAF Wittering	Rolled over on landing
02/12	Tornado GR1	ZA610	617 Sqn	Nr Flamborough Head	Flew into sea at night while attempting air-to-air refuelling with Buccaneer buddy tanker; 2F

1986					
Date	Type	Serial	Unit	Location	Cause
02/01	Lynx AH1	XZ606	665 Sqn	NI	Heavy landing, vortex ring
07/01	Phantom FGR2	XV434	29 Sqn	20nm NW Harrogate	Abandoned following loss of control at low-level; Ej
20/03	Lynx AH1	XZ213	AAC	WG	Flew into trees following engine failure in helarm position
25/03	Wasp HAS1	XT439	–	Merryfield	Crashed following loss of control
16/04	Sea Harrier FRS1	XZ491	801 Sqn	Nr Benbecula	Abandoned over sea after running out of fuel; Ej
29/04	Gazelle AH1	XX336	3Flt	North Yorkshire	Crashed following wirestrike
13/05	Chinook HC1	ZA715	1310 Flt	Mt Young, Falkland Is	Flew into high ground in whiteout; 3F
25/05	Vampire T11	XH304	Vintage Pair	RAF Mildenhall	Abandoned following mid-air collision; Ej
25/05	Meteor T7	WA669	Vintage Pair	RAF Mildenhall	Crashed following mid-air collision, 2F
06/06	Jet Provost T5A	XW407	7FTS	Helmsley, N Yorks	Abandoned following mid-air collision during tail-chase; Ej
06/06	Jet Provost T5A	XW411	7FTS	Helmsley, N Yorks	Abandoned following mid-air collision during tail-chase; Ej
17/06	Harrier GR3	XW769;	–	RNAS Yeovilton	Abandoned on finals following fuel leak; Ej
19/06	Victor K2	XL191	55 Sqn	Hamilton, Canada	Undershot approach; DBR
28/06	Harrier GR3	XW769	4 Sqn	Chièvres AB, Belgium	Crashed following loss of control at low-level during air display; 1F

Lynx AH1 XZ213, 20 March 1986.

25 May 1986: Meteor T7 WA669 and Vampire T11 XH304

Circumstances:
On 25 May 1986, the RAF Vintage Pair Display Team were engaged in an air display at RAF Mildenhall which was to include the Meteor leading the Vampire in a formation line-astern barrel roll to the left. The display went well until the aircraft reached the top of the formation barrel roll when the Vampire was unable to match the Meteor's rate of roll and became displaced down, left and slightly back from the line-astern position. The Vampire then moved forward, passed underneath the Meteor, and climbed turning slightly to the right. The Vampire's starboard rudder, fin and elevator struck the Meteor's port engine nacelle nosing which separated from the aircraft and fell clear. The Vampire's starboard rudder detached and fell clear.

After the collision, the Vampire pitched up and the two crew ejected successfully. The Meteor, which was not fitted with ejection seats, struck the ground shortly after the mid-air collision and the two crew were killed. Both aircraft were destroyed.

Cause:
The investigation established that, although the Meteor pilot's flying of the barrel roll may have made maintaining formation difficult, the Vampire pilot could have avoided the subsequent collision by turning away to the left. Appropriate action has been taken in respect of the Vampire's pilot.

Claims:
Claims have been paid for crop damage as a result of this accident.

Meteor T7 WA669 and Vampire T11 XH304, 25 May 1986. *David Oliver*

Above and below:
Victor K2 XL191 of No 55 Squadron which crashed in Canada on 19 June 1986. The aircraft undershot its approach to the runway at Hamilton and was damaged beyond repair.
C. Sloat, Crown Copyright

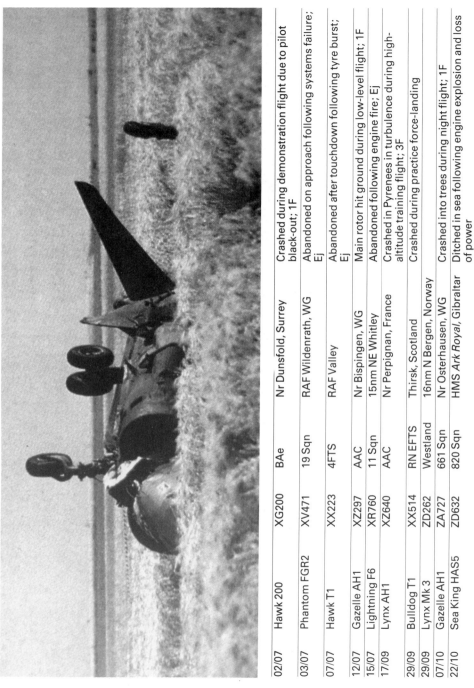

Harrier GR3 XW769, 28 June 1986. *David Oliver*

02/07	Hawk 200	XG200	BAe	Nr Dunsfold, Surrey	Crashed during demonstration flight due to pilot black-out; 1F
03/07	Phantom FGR2	XV471	19 Sqn	RAF Wildenrath, WG	Abandoned on approach following systems failure; Ej
07/07	Hawk T1	XX223	4FTS	RAF Valley	Abandoned after touchdown following tyre burst; Ej
12/07	Gazelle AH1	XZ297	AAC	Nr Bispingen, WG	Main rotor hit ground during low-level flight; 1F
15/07	Lightning F6	XR760	11 Sqn	15nm NE Whitley	Abandoned following engine fire; Ej
17/09	Lynx AH1	XZ640	AAC	Nr Perpignan, France	Crashed in Pyrenees in turbulence during high-altitude training flight; 3F
29/09	Bulldog T1	XX514	RN EFTS	Thirsk, Scotland	Crashed during practice force-landing
29/09	Lynx Mk 3	ZD262	Westland	16nm N Bergen, Norway	
07/10	Gazelle AH1	ZA727	661 Sqn	Nr Osterhausen, WG	Crashed into trees during night flight; 1F
22/10	Sea King HAS5	ZD632	820 Sqn	HMS *Ark Royal*, Gibraltar	Ditched in sea following engine explosion and loss of power

Date	Type	Serial	Unit	Location	Remarks
03/11	Hawk T1	XX297	CFS	RAF Scampton	Abandoned on approach following flame-out during aerobatic practice (Red Arrows); Ej
04/11	Wessex HU5	XS518	85 Sqn	Limassol Bay, Cyprus	Flew into sea at night on CASEVAC, 3F
27/11	Jaguar GR1A	XX732	226 OCU	Nr Hawick, Scotland	Flew into ground during low-level flight (USAF pilot); 1F
02/12	Tornado GR1	ZA555	TWCU	Nr Diss, Norfolk	Abandoned following engine failure; Ej
05/12	Hawk T1	–	1TWU	RAF Brawdy	Abandoned during approach; Ej
10/12	Tornado GR1	ZA605	617 Sqn	Thorney, Cambridge	Abandoned following mid-air collision; Ej
10/12	Tornado GR1	ZA611	617 Sqn	Thorney, Cambridge	Abandoned following mid-air collision; Ej

Bulldog T1 XX514, 29 September 1986. *Crown Copyright*

1987

Date	Type	Serial	Unit	Location	Cause
01/02	Wessex HC2	XT674	22 Sqn	Mt Ben More, Perthshire	Crashed on take-off at night in snow storm during mountain rescue; 1F
24/02	Sea King HAS5	XV668	706 Sqn	Nr Falmouth	Flew into sea at night; 3F
27/02	Chinook HC1	ZA721	78 Sqn	RAF Mt Pleasant, Falkland Is	Crashed following loss of control during test flight; 7F
18/03	Lynx AH1	XZ204	653 Sqn	Nr Sallern, WG	Crashed following tail rotor gearbox failure; 2F
19/03	Lightning F3	XP707	LTF	Nr RAF Binbrook	Crashed during aerobatic practice; Ej
29/03	Tornado GR1	ZA412	20 Sqn	RAF Wildenrath, WG	Crashed on landing when nosewheel hit barrier
22/04	Buccaneer S2	XW540	12 Sqn	Nr Wick, Scotland	Flew into sea at night; 2F
03/06	Tornado GR1	ZA366	TWCU	Nr Manby, Lincs	Abandoned following power failure; Ej
17/06	Tornado GR1	ZA493	20 Sqn	6nm S Keswick, Cumbria	Abandoned following mid-air collision; Ej
17/06	Jaguar GR1A	XZ116	41 Sqn	6nm S Keswick, Cumbria	Crashed following mid-air collision; 1F
24/06	Jaguar GR1A	XZ386	226 OCU	Nr Builth Wells, Wales	Crashed following loss of control during practice bounce; Ej; 1F
01/07	Lightning F6	XR763	5 Sqn	RAF Akrotiri, Cyprus	Abandoned on approach following double engine failure; Ej
16/07	Gazelle AH1	ZA731	BATUS	Suffield Range, Canada	Tail hit ground during exercise; 1F
22/07	Sea King Mk 42B		Westland	St Raphaël, France	Ditched in the Mediterranean Sea during sonar dipping tests
27/07	Tornado GR1	ZD738	31 Sqn	Sadmoor, Yorkshire	Abandoned at low-level following control lock; Ej
26/08	Phantom F-4J	ZE358	74 Sqn	Trefenter, 10nw SW Aberystwyth	Flew into high ground during low-level training flight; 2F
07/09	Phantom FG1	XT861	43 Sqn	North Sea	Abandoned over the sea following a mid-air collision with Phantom in five-ship formation; Ej
11/09	Nimrod MR2	XV236	42 Sqn	RAF St Mawgan	Undercarriage collapsed on landing
16/10	Wessex HU5	XT461	771 Sqn	Nr Porthleven, Cornwall	Ditched in sea following engine failure
18/10	Sea Harrier FRS1	ZA190	801 Sqn	HMS *Ark Royal*	Abandoned over Irish Sea following fire caused by birdstrike; Ej
22/10	Harrier GR5	ZD325	BAe	250nm SW Ireland	Crashed into sea following involuntary bale-out by pilot over Salisbury Plain; 1F

27 Feb 1987: Chinook HC1 ZA721

Circumstances:
On 27 February 1987, Chinook ZA721 was prepared at RAF Mount Pleasant on the Falklands for a full flight test following servicing and a structural repair. Ground runs and hover checks had been completed satisfactorily the previous day. In addition to the normal crew, the helicopter carried four technical NCOs, two operating the rotor-tune equipment, one under instruction on the rotor-tune and one recording engine vibration data.

The Chinook took-off, transitioned and climbed west along the runway, turned right and passed north and east of the runway before continuing outbound to the southeast. The aircraft flew southeasterly at normal cruise speed at a height between 300 and 700ft. Shortly afterwards, from straight and level flight on a northwesterly heading, the nose began to dip at a moderate rate until the aircraft assumed a very steep, possibly vertical, dive.

A short, unintelligible radio transmission from the Chinook was recorded on the Air Traffic Control tape and the aircraft hit the ground immediately afterwards some 6km southeast of the airfield. An eyewitness at the Air Traffic Control Centre initiated the rescue services and on arrival at the crash site it was immediately apparent to the Search and Rescue helicopter crew that the aircraft had disintegrated on impact and had been almost totally consumed by a subsequent fire. There were no survivors.

Cause:
Little evidence could be obtained from the brief and garbled final radio call, and eyewitnesses were only able to report seeing the aircraft tilt nose down and fly into the ground. However, during the course of its investigation, the Inquiry was able to eliminate operating and natural hazards, engine/ major structural failure as well as disorientation and aircrew error as possible causes.

Examination of the wreckage showed that the aft Longitudinal Cyclic Trim Actuator (LCTA) clutch had failed, preventing the LCTA from extending once retracted. Flight loads could not have caused the LCTA to retract, therefore it was most likely to have been retracted either automatically on take-off or manually by the pilot while following the flight test schedule. However, the effects of a failure of an aft LCTA to extend from fully retracted would then have been easily contained by the pilot unless something, such as another flying control defect, prevented him from so doing. Simulator experiments showed that, under such circumstances, the estimated impact speed of 150kt could be achieved from a height of 700ft if the starting speed was about 120kt.

The forward swivelling Upper Boost

RAF Chinook HC1 ZA717 which crashed in the Falkland Islands 25/7/89. *David Oliver*

Actuator (UBA) showed an extension of 180mm which is less than expected under the circumstances. When the actuator was dismantled it was found that, during manufacture, the controlling spool valve had not been locked to the threaded input control rod. Moreover, the internal bore of the spool had been machined at an angle to the spool axis so that transverse 'g' loads caused by vibration could turn the spool, screwing it along the control rod. When dismantled, the spool was found to be displaced along the rod by $\frac{1}{10}$ turn from the normal position. The Inquiry determined that the spool valve displacement of $\frac{1}{2}$ to two turns from the normal position would result in a very slow rate of extension of the actuator, tending towards a jam at 2-3$\frac{1}{2}$ turns.

Following a practical test the Inquiry decided that if the pilot had applied a rapid control input, in response to some unidentified nose-down pitch attitude change, at a moment when the spool valve was considerably displaced along its control rod, then the UBA could have jammed with an extension of about 180mm. The failed aft LCTA position would have produced a flight path resembling that reported by eyewit-nesses. Thus the Inquiry considered that a possible cause of the accident was jamming of the forward swivelling UBA by spool migration with LCTA malfunction as a likely contributory cause. However, the valve position found after the impact was inconsistent with this cause and prevented the Inquiry from attributing the accident conclusively to it.

Due to lack of evidence the Inquiry could not completely discount a number of other possible causes. These included disconnection or failure of a control run, hydraulic return line blockage, loose article hazard and crew incapacitation or physiological problem.

Subsequent actions:
All RAF Chinook UBA spool valves were inspected as soon as the condition of the valve on ZA721 became known. All new valves are now inspected upon receipt.

Consideration is being given to the fitting of an ADR and Crash Locator Beacon to the aircraft. Action is in hand to obtain a full Design Authority hazard analysis of the flying controls and associated systems.

2 Nov 1987: Harrier GR3s XV790 and XZ136

Circumstances:

The pilots of XV790 and XZ136 were briefed as Nos 3 and 4 of a formation of six Harriers based at RAF Gutersloh, West Germany. The formation planned to carry out a co-ordinated attack on Otterburn Range. From an initial reference point, even-numbered aircraft were to follow an almost direct track to the target while odd-numbered aircraft were to take a slightly longer offset route to achieve a sequenced separation of aircraft over the target. The attack order was to be 2, 1, 4, 3, 6, 5.

The sortie progressed as planned and the formation elements arrived at the reference point in the correct order. No 2 overflew the target and No 1 attacked 8sec later. After a delay of 16sec, No 3 (XV790) and 4 (XZ136) attacked simultaneously. The aircraft collided almost directly over the target and hit the ground very shortly afterwards. Both pilots were killed instantly and the aircraft destroyed.

Causes:

The accident was seen by several eyewitnesses and recorded on video, and the investigation was able to discount the weather or other natural operating hazards. Both aircraft appeared to be under control until the collision and pilot incapacitation was therefore improbable.

By the nature of the attack plan, small differences in speed or track during the attack run could have accounted for the aircraft arriving over the target simultaneously, although failure to achieve the desired separation should not in itself have caused an accident. However, it was considered distraction could have played a part. Confusion over collision avoidance was also a possibility and either pilot may have been deceived in some manner into the belief that it was safe to continue his attack.

The investigation concluded that the cause of the accident was that the pilots failed to avoid each other as briefed. A contributory cause was that the attack plan contained hidden flaws: it was conceived as a visual plan — in effect it was not; it required a degree of precision in its execution which, in the event, was difficult to achieve; the final safety measure of briefed collision avoidance responsibilities was vulnerable to compromise through distraction or deception.

Subsequent action:

Separation criteria and procedures for Harrier attacks have been reviewed.

Date	Type	Serial	Unit	Location	Cause
23/10	Gazelle AH1	XX457	AAC	Middle Wallop	Main rotor blade hit ground during practice sloping ground landing
02/11	Harrier GR3	XV790	3 Sqn	Otterburn Range	Mid-air collision with a Harrier at low-level during exercise; 1F
02/11	Harrier GR3	XZ136	3 Sqn	Otterburn Range	Mid-air collision with a Harrier at low-level during exercise; 1F (US Navy pilot)
11/11	Harrier GR3	XV747	233 OCU	RAF Wittering	Abandoned on landing; Ej
16/11	Hawk T1	XX241	CFS	Melton, Lincs	Abandoned following mid-air collision with Hawk during formation practice (Red Arrows); Ej
16/11	Hawk T1A	XX259	CFS	Melton, Lincs	Abandoned following mid-air collision with Hawk during formation practice (Red Arrows); Ej
25/11	Gazelle HT2	XW891	705 Sqn	Culdrose	Crashed during training sortie

1988

Date	Type	Serial	Unit	Location	Cause
13/01	Wessex HC2	XT607	72 Sqn	Crawfordsburn, NI	Force-landed near hospital
22/01	Hawk T1A	XX243	CFS	RAF Scampton	Crashed on airfield during formation training flight; 1F
03/02	Sea King HAS5	XV652	826 Sqn	Nr Barcelona, Spain	Ditched in sea and sank while operating from HMIMS *Poolster*
02/03	Bulldog T1	XX712	Manchester UAS	Nr Southport	Crashed on beach during solo training flight; 1F
10/03	Lynx HAS3	XZ243	702 Sqn	48nm W of Cabo Roca, Portugal	Crashed into sea during night approach to RFA *Engadine*; 2F
29/03	Tornado GR1	ZA448	15 Sqn	Nellis AFB, USA	Abandoned over desert range during Exercise 'Green Flag'; Ej
11/04	Lightning F6	XR769	11 Sqn	5nm E of Easington, Lincs	Abandoned over the sea following engine failure; Ej
20/04	Phantom FG1	XR769	43 Sqn	North Sea 28nm E of Leuchars	Crashed into sea during Exercise 'Elder Forest'; 2F
06/05	Chinook HC1	ZA672	18 Sqn	Hannover Airport, WG	Crashed into gangway pier while hover taxying; 2F

11 April 1988: Lightning F6, XR769

(The last RAF Lightning crash)

Circumstances:

On the morning of 11 April 1988, the pilot of XR769 was carrying out a routine training mission as the No 2 of a formation of four Binbrook-based Lightnings. The sortie proceeded without incident for the first 1hr 30min. At this point the pilot, having cancelled reheat, slowly retarded the throttles in the cold power range. A series of loud bangs ensued and the pilot immediately advanced the throttles slightly and initiated a pull up in an attempt to clear the condition. However, the 'FIRE' caption light illuminated and a small amount of fumes and smoke entered the cockpit but these quickly cleared. He declared a 'Mayday', continued a steep climb and closed down the No 1 engine. He requested a visual inspection from the formation leader and levelled the aircraft at approximately 10,000ft heading towards Binbrook. The formation leader reported what appeared to be fuel venting from the aircraft.

When the aircraft was some 53 miles northeast of Binbrook the 'FIRE 1' caption extinguished. However, the formation leader reported fire issuing from the port side of the fuselage above the Red Top drill round. The fire continued to spread and the pilot turned the aircraft away from the coast, completed pre-ejection drills and initiated ejection. The pilot's ejection was successful and he landed safely in the water before being rescued by helicopter after only 15min in the sea.

Cause:

The investigation considered that the evidence was sufficiently compelling to discount all but that of persistent fire and structural damage as a result of an uncontained failure of the No 1 engine following a severe surge, as the probable cause of the accident. However, in the absence of any wreckage, a degree of conjecture was inevitable concerning the exact cause of the surge.

XR769 of No 11 Squadron — the last Lightning to crash. *MAP*

Date	Type	Serial	Unit	Location	Cause
10/05	Tornado GR1	ZD808	17 Sqn	Nr Osnabrück, WG	Crashed into houses during low-level training flight; 2F
13/05	Hawk T1A	XX197	1TWU	RAF Brawdy	Abandoned following engine failure on take-off; Ej
20/05	Harrier GR3	XV809	3 Sqn	RAF Gutersloh, WG	Crashed into house on take-off after entering low cloud; 1F (Flt Lt Paul Adams)
30/05	Meteor T7	WF791	CFS	Near Bagington Airport, Coventry	Crashed during air display following lowering of u/c while airbrakes out in circuit; 1F (Flt Lt Peter Stacey)
14/06	Hunter GA11	WT809	FRADU	Nr Ilchester, Somerset	Crashed in Yeovil circuit following engine failure; Ej
23/06	Lynx AH1	XZ664	665 Sqn	South Armagh, NI	Force-landed after being hit by IRA small arms fire
24/06	Hawk T1A	XX304	CFS	RAF Scampton, Lincs	Abandoned on take-off following power failure (Red Arrows); Ej
02/08	Phantom FGR2	XV501	56 Sqn	Mayenne, France	Abandoned during training flight following technical failure; Ej
09/08	Tornado GR1	ZA329	TTTE	Nr Milburn, Cumbria	Crashed during night training flight following mid-air collision with another Tornado; 2F
09/08	Tornado GR1	ZA593	617 Sqn	Nr Milburn, Cumbria	Crashed during night training flight following mid-air collision with another Tornado; 2F
18/08	Harrier GR3	XW921	3 Sqn	RAF Gutersloh, WG	Abandoned on approach; Ej
07/09	Jaguar T2A	XX834	6 Sqn	Nr Wildbad-Kreuth, WG	Crashed after hitting HT wires; Pilot F; USAF back-seater Ej
23/09	Phantom FGR2	XV428	228 OCU	RAF Abingdon	Crashed on airfield following failure to recover from loop during air display practice; 2F
13/10	Sea King HAS5	XZ916	826 Sqn	15nm off Plymouth	Crashed into the sea during an approach to RFA Resource; 2F; 2I
18/10	Phantom FGR2	XV437	92 Sqn	Nr Holzminden, WG	Abandoned during training flight following technical failure; Ej

1989

Date	Type	Serial	Unit	Location	Cause
09/01	Phantom FGR2	XT908	228 OCU	North Sea 50nm off Dundee, Scotland	Crashed into sea during training sortie; 2Ej, 1F
13/01	Tornado GR1	ZD891	14 Sqn	Nr Wiesmoor, WG	Crashed following mid-air collision with formation of WGAF Alpha Jets on approach to Wittmund; 2F

30 May 1988: Meteor T7 WF791

Circumstances:

On 30 May 1988 the pilot of Meteor WF791 took-off from RAF Scampton for a display during the Warwickshire Air Pageant at Coventry airport. The weather was good, visibility 30km with 3/7 cloud at 2,500ft. The display followed the normal, sequence for about 3min until a wingover to the right, which was intended to bring the aircraft back along the display line with undercarriage and flaps extended. However, although the manoeuvres up to this point seemed normal, the Meteor had been flown throughout the sequence with airbrakes extended, contrary to normal practice.

As the pilot commenced the wingover, flaps were at about ¼ and airbrakes were extended. The undercarriage appeared to lower normally as the Meteor climbed to the highest point of the wingover to the right. As the aircraft began the descending turn back to the airfield, the roll rate appeared faster than on previous occasions, the bank increased to 45° and the nose dropped. The aircraft turned rapidly through 90° to the right and settled into a dive, with the nose some 45° below the horizon and the wings approximately level. This attitude remained fairly constant, apart from small variations in the bank, until shortly before impact, when a roll to the right developed. The aircraft crashed into an area of open ground close to the airfield and was destroyed.

The Meteor was not fitted with ejection seats and there was insufficient height or time for successful abandonment. The airport Fire Services were at the scene within 8min and extinguished small residual fires. It was

established that the pilot had died instantly on impact.

Cause:

Video recordings and photographs of the Meteor show that much, and probably all, of the display had been flown with the airbrakes extended. Examination of the wreckage indicated that the airbrakes were extended on impact. However, the Meteor T7 Pilot's notes include the following: 'If the aircraft is yawed at speeds below 170kt with the airbrakes out, the nose may drop suddenly and the elevators become ineffective until the yaw is removed or the airbrakes retracted. The

Meteor T7 WF971 crashed during an air display at Baginton airport, Coventry, 30 May 1988.
Duncan Cubitt

tendency is aggravated if the ventral tank is fitted. Airbrakes should not be used at airspeeds below 170kt at circuit height and should be in before the undercarriage is lowered.'

This phenomenon, colloquially known as the 'Phantom Dive', is due to airflow being disturbed at high angle of attacks by turbulence from the airbrakes, and such disturbances would be increased by sideslip. The directional stability of the Meteor T7 is less than that of earlier marks of Meteor because of the increased nose and canopy size, and directional stability is further degraded by the ventral tank and the nosewheel when extended. Any side-slip at conditions of marginal directional stability would increase this effect and result in loss of elevator and rudder effectiveness and a nose-down pitch.

When Meteor WF791 began to roll right into its final dive, the aircraft was at its lowest speed in the display, probably around 150kt, had its undercarriage down and airbrakes extended. The investigation considered that all of the criteria required for a 'Phantom Dive' were present and that the aircraft entered an undemanded dive, due to airbrakes being extended at low speed. There was no evidence of any pre-crash defect in the aircraft's airbrake system.

Tornado GR1 ZD891, 13 January 1989. *Reuter*

13 Jan 1989: Tornado GR1 ZD891

Circumstances:

At approximately 08.53Z on 13 January 1989, a No 14 Squadron RAF Tornado GR1, ZD891, collided with a German Air Force Alpha Jet, 40+87, south of the village of Wiesmoor in West Germany. The Tornado was one of a stream of aircraft flying a pre-planned route. The Alpha Jet was the lead aircraft of a four-aircraft tactical formation, tasked as the leading element of an eight-aircraft package to carry out simulated attacks on the GAF airbase at Wittmund. Both the Tornado and the Alpha Jet were destroyed in the collision. Although the pilot of the German aircraft was able to eject safely, the Torando crew was killed.

ZD891 had taken-off from RAF Brüggen at 08.10Z as the 23rd mission of a planned 30 aircraft launch on the last day of a station exercise. Once airborne, the crew were required to route through a holding pattern and a timing gate so as not to conflict with other participating aircraft before carrying out a simulated attack against a field target in German Low Flying Area (LFA) 5. After this target, common westerly routing across the North German Plain was planned to achieve 1min separation between aircraft before the timed 'first-run' attacks at Nordhorn range and a pre-planned, sequenced recovery to Brüggen.

The Tornado crew flew through the timing gate and attacked the field target in LFA5, both on time. Having exited the LFA at its northwest corner, they took a westerly heading for the next turning point, some 4nm northwest of the town of Brake. Established now on the same route as the other participating Tornados, they turned on to a heading of 270°T. Shortly afterwards, approximately 2nm south of the village of Wiesmor, ZD891 struck Alpha Jet 40+87. At the moment of collision, the Tornado was flying straight and level at 465kt IAS and 500ft above the ground.

The Alpha Jet, as lead of a four-aircraft formation, had taken-off from WGAF airbase Oldenburg at approximately 08.25Z. After a short route over the North German Plain, the four aircraft overflew a planned turning point near the town of Friesoythe before taking up northerly headings towards their Initial Points (IPs) for the final attack run against Wittmund airfields. The formation, with Nos 3 and 4 accelerated from 360kt to 400kt on this leg.

Approximately 2min before his IP, and 1min before the collision, the pilot of Alpha Jet 40+87 noted that he was about 1nm to the left of his planned track. He therefore made a small heading change of 3 or 4 degrees to the right and rolled out on 004°T. On turning his head to the right to check the position of his No 2, he became fleetingly aware of another aircraft at extremely close quarters, just aft of his aircraft. He ejected successfully, sustaining minor burns to the lower part of both legs and back injuries consistent with the ejection. One or two seconds before the collision, the pilot of the No 2 Alpha Jet saw an aircraft in his 12-1 o'clock position at very close range. He pulled 5.3g in an attempt to avoid a collision, experiencing abrupt wing rock and yaw either as a result of the snatch pull or from the Tornado's slipstream. After avoiding the Tornado, he looked down to the left and saw a fireball on the ground, although he initially believed it to be coming from his left drop tank because of his line of sight. He declared an emergency and landed at Wittmund where his aircraft was subsequently found to be undamaged.

Examination of the aircraft wreckage revealed that the first point of contact in the collision had been between the

Tornado's radome and the front lower section of the Alpha Jet's starboard drop tank. (The drop tank had been mounted on the Alpha Jet's outer wing station). Thereafter, the upper front fuselage and cockpit area of the Tornado had cut through the starboard wing and outboard pylon, the aft fuselage and tailplane assembly of the Alpha Jet. Neither Tornado crew member had made any attempt to eject and death was instantaneous.

The information available from the voice track of the Tornado's Accident Data Recorder (ADR), together with the statements of the four Alpha Jet pilots, revealed that none of the five crews involved had seen the impending collision in time to prevent it. Neither the Tornado pilot nor his navigator had seen any of the Alpha Jets at all. The No 2 pilot of the Alpha Jet formation had seen the Tornado at such a late stage he was forced to take violent avoiding action with no time to transmit a warning, while the leader had had only a fleeting glimpse of the Tornado prior to impact. The other two Alpha Jet pilots had not seen the Tornado at all as it had passed across the noses from right to left at an approximate range of 4nm.

Cause:
In considering the failure of the crews to see each other, it was possible to discount both the weather and sun position as contributory factors. At the time of the accident, the weather and visibility were well in excess of the prescribed minima, with no significant cloud and an out-of-sun visibility of 8-14km. The sun, on an azimuth of 140°, was aft of the beam position for all the aircraft involved. Consequently, the effects of aircraft conspicuity, visual acuity, physical obscuration and workload on the crews' lookout were

assessed. Although the Tornado is considerably larger than the Alpha Jet, both aircraft represent small targets at the ranges required to ensure timely visual contact. Moreover, the Tornado and four Alpha Jets involved in the accident were camouflaged in paint schemes optimised to reduce to a minimum their conspicuousness at low level, while red low intensity strobe anti-collision lights, with which all the aircraft were equipped, would have done little to counteract this effect in the prevailing light conditions.

The human eye is ill-equipped to detect small stationary objects unless they appear directly ahead in the field of view. Displacement of an image from the centre of the retina (the fovea) causes an exponential decrease in visual acuity. For example, a displacement of 5° from the fovea occasions a 75% loss in visual acuity, while at a displacement of 45° the loss is 95%.

The extent of the physical obscuration caused by the metal canopy arches of the Tornado and Alpha Jet, assuming a fixed head and 'normal' eye position was determined. For the Alpha Jet, the 'worst' case blind arcs were between 30° and 50° relative to the aircraft's longitudinal axis while, for the Tornado, the arcs were between 30° and 53° for the pilot and between 36° and 45° for the navigator. Clearly, any change in head position from the assumed datum would change the pattern of this obscuration. As the two aircraft converged towards the collision, the relative bearing of the Alpha Jet from the Tornado was 40° left from the longitudinal axis, while that of the Tornado from the Alpha Jet was 47° to the right.

The effect of conflicting and competing workload priorities on the lookout of the crews was considered. The four Alpha Jets were preparing to attack

Wittmund airfield. This may have concentrated their lookout in the 12 o'clock as they tried to identify their PIs. Certainly the workload of the Nos 1 and 2 was increasing with the No 2 concentrating much of his lookout towards his IP and to the left, towards his leader. Analysis of the Tornado's ADR and its voice track suggests that, in the seconds before the collision, the navigator was probably 'head-in' taking a radar fix prior to the attack at Nordhorn while the pilot's attention may have been concentrated on the Head-Up Display (HUD), either to check weapon symbology or to monitor aircraft height. In the 3min prior to the accident, the pilot had made several auto-pilot selections on the Auto-pilot and Flight Director System (AFDS) control panel. Although this would have detracted from the pilot's lookout scan, there was nothing to suggest that he had been distracted in any way 30sec prior to the collision.

Both aircraft were equipped with radar altimeters with height read-outs displayed in their HUDs. Over the flat North German Plain it was relatively simple for the pilots to maintain their height datum with precision. This considerably reduced the chances of the two aircraft being separated vertically. At the same time of the collision the overall width of the Alpha Jet formation was between 3.5 and 4nm and the fore and aft spacing was approximately 1.5nm. The formation was flying at right angles to the track of a stream of Tornados planned to be 7nm apart. This geometry significantly increased the statistical chances of a collision between the Alpha Jet formation and the stream of Tornados. In conclusion, the cause of the collision was the failure of the pilots involved to take avoiding action on each other because they did not see each other in time. However, despite the fundamental requirement to 'see and avoid', an exceptional combination of significant factors conspired to make the two pilots lookout task unusually difficult. Action to emphasise the overriding and fundamental need to lookout is in hand. High Intensity Strobe Lights will be fitted to Tornados as a priority. In the future, it has been arranged with the appropriate NATO tasking agency that they will issue Airspace Activity Warnings when launches of large numbers of aircraft are planned.

ZD891 — another victim of a mid-air collision. *MAP*

8 Mar 1989: Jet Provost T3A XN547

Circumstances:

A student pilot on a solo general handling sortie in a Jet Provost T3A lost control of the aircraft during an aerobatic sequence being performed at about 9,000ft and was unable to recover the aircraft to normal flight, the aircraft descended rapidly and the pilot decided to eject as he approached 5,000ft. He landed successfully by parachute and the aircraft crashed in open farmland. The pilot was relatively inexperienced, but he had been briefed, and had previously practised with an instructor the exercises he was undertaking.

The aerobatic sequence proceeded normally until a stall turn to the left was attempted. The aircraft was slightly right wing low in the vertical and failed to yaw left in spite of full rudder. At a point when the airspeed decayed to zero the pilot correctly centralised the controls. The aircraft hammerheaded forwards and fell through the vertical to an inverted position from which it yawed violently, the pilot diagnosed that he was in an inverted spin and took recommended recovery action. However, the aircraft continued to spin and he abandoned the aircraft when he realised the height remaining was insufficient to execute recovery.

Cause:

The accident was caused because the student pilot inadvertently induced an entry to an inverted spin from which he could not recover in the height available. After the vertical stall caused by the failed stall turn in the aerobatic sequence, the aircraft pitched forward through the downward vertical to an inverted position at an attitude of 30° to the horizontal.

The pilot had relieved the control buffet during this manoeuvre by moving the control column slightly forward. Unfortunately this position of the controls held the aircraft momentarily in an inverted stall from which it departed into an inverted spin.

The subsequent aircraft motion was very disorientating and visual clues were conflicting with no horizon from the inverted position. The pilot was experiencing negative 'g' and although he believed his control positions were neutral, he was holding a small input to down elevator during the descent which was sufficient to prevent the aircraft recovering from the inverted spin.

The inverted spin is not a practised exercise and the introduction of such a thoroughly disorientating manoeuvre is not recommended as part of the training programme. The importance of regular briefings on the correct recovery actions from an incipient inverted spin have been re-emphasised. The immediate action of centralising the control will recover the aircraft and there is no justification for any change to this drill.

XZ585, a Sea King HAR3 of No 202 Squadron, crashed near Fort William, 28 January 1989.
Miller Harris

28/01	Sea King HAR3	XZ585	202 Sqn	Nr Lock Laggan, Fort William, Scotland	Crashed on high ground following main rotor gearbox failure
08/03	Jet Provost T3A	XN547	1FTS	Nr Great Habton, North Yorks	Abandoned following loss of control in inverted spin; Ej
13/04	Jaguar GR1	XZ359	54 Sqn	St Abbs Head, Berwickshire, Scotland	Crashed into cliff during low-level training sortie; 1F
24/04	Phantom FGR2	XT893	56 Sqn	North Sea 48nm off Flamborough Head	Crashed into sea following technical failure; 2Ej
25/04	Bulldog T1	XX517	1FTS	Nr Catterick, North Yorks	Abandoned following loss of control during aerobatic training due to disorientation
08/05	Jetstream T2	XX489	750 Sqn	Sea off Plymouth, Devon	Crashed into sea during demonstration flight following engine failure; 3F
18/05	Lynx HAS3GM	XZ244	HMS *Brilliant*	Sea of Mombasa, Kenya	Crashed into sea while ferrying ship's crew ashore following loss of cabin door in flight; 9F
10/06	Sea Fury FB11	TF956	FAA Historic Flight	Nr Prestwick, Scotland	Abandoned over sea following hydraulic failure locked one wheel down and one up, preventing safe landing

XZ451, a Sea Harrier FRS1 of No 801 Squadron, RN, crashed into the Mediterranean on 30 November 1989. *Air Britain*

Date	Type	Serial	Unit	Location	Cause
14/06	Hawk T1	XX182	4FTS	Borth, Wales	Crashed following a mid-air collision with second Hawk during training flight; Ej
14/06	Hawk T1	XX291	4FTS	Borth, Wales	Crashed following mid-air collision with Hawk XX182; 1F
20/06	Harrier T4A	XW925	4 Sqn	RAF Gutersloh, WG	Crashed on approach; 1F, 1Ej
20/07	Tornado GR1	ZA468	15 Sqn	RAF Laarbruch, WG	Abandoned after take-off; Ej
21/07	Tornado F3	–	23 Sqn	North Sea off Sunderland	Abandoned over the sea following mechanical failure; 1Ej, 1F
24/07	Chinook HC1	–	–	RAF Odiham, Hants	Crashed from low hover following gearbox failure
25/07	Chinook HC1	ZA717	78 Sqn	RAF Mount Pleasant, Falklands	Crashed from hover following gearbox failure. Chinook fleet grounded for checks
01/08	Lynx AH7	ZE377	657 Sqn	Bodney Camp, Norfolk	Crashed and burnt out; 4F, 4I
14/09	Tornado GR1	ZD710	14 Sqn	Nr Drayton, Oxon	Abandoned after take-off from RAF Abingdon following birdstrike; 1F
20/09	Hawk T1A	XX192	1TWU	RAF Brawdy, Wales	Crashed on take-off following engine failure; 2F
04/10	Sea Harrier FRS1	ZA191	801 Sqn	HMS Ark Royal, Lyme Bay	Abandoned over the sea following collision with carrier's mast during low-level exercise; Ej
27/10	Sea King HAS5	XZ582	814 Sqn	HMS Invincible, Atlantic Ocean	Ditched in sea and sank following engine failure
30/11	Sea Harrier FRS1	XZ451	801 Sqn	Mediterranean Sea off Sardinia	Crashed into sea; Ej

1990

Date	Type	Serial	Unit	Location	Cause
09/01	Tornado GR1A	ZA394	2 Sqn	Spadeadam Range	Abandoned following a mid-air collision with a Jaguar GR1A; Ej
11/02	Gazelle AH1	–	AAC	Nr Augher, Co Tyrone, NI	Shot down during border patrol by IRA groundfire; 2I
21/02	Hunter T8C	XF358	FRADU	RNAS Yeovilton	Crashed during emergency landing
22/02	Tucano T51	ZH203	Shorts	Off Mull of Kintyre	Crashed into sea (First accident of type); 1F
28/02	Sea Harrier FRS1	XZ495	899 Sqn	RNAS Yeovilton	Crashed on landing following undershoot

10/04	Hunter T8C	XF985	FRADU	Nr Charminster, Dorset	Abandoned following engine failure; Ej
30/04	Shackleton AEW2	WR965	8 Sqn	Is of Harris, South Hebrides	Crashed into high ground in fog during routine training flight; 10F
30/04	Tornado GR1A	ZA454	15 Sqn	Goose Bay, Canada	Abandoned during routine training flight following engine fire; Ej
08/05	Sea Harrier FRS1	XZ460	800 Sqn	Mediterranean off Sardinia	Crashed into sea during Exercise 'Dragon Hammer'' 1F
09/05	Hawk T1	XX347	4FTS	Anglesey	Abandoned during training flight; Ej
17/06	Lynx HAS3	–	829 Sqn	North Sea	Fell off the flight deck of a frigate following the breakage of the 'harpoon' restraint
27/06	Canberra	WH972	100 Sqn	3nm S of Kinloss	Crashed into field on approach to Kinloss on routine training sortie in bad weather; 1F

Army Air Corps Gazelle AH1 shot down by the IRA while on border patrol, 11 February 1990.
Crispin Rodwell

WH965, a Shackleton AEW2, crashed in fog on the Isle of Harris, 30 April 1990.
Donald MacPherson

Types Lost Cat 5: 1966-90

	1966	1967	1968	1969	1970	1971	1972	1973	1974	1975	1976	1977
Lightning	7	6	4	1	8	10	5	4	3	1	1	1
Jet Provost	8	1	3	3	4	3	1	2			1	1
Sea Vixen	9	2	3	2	2	1		1				
Javelin	6	4	1									
Gnat	4	3	2	5	2	3	2	3		2	4	
Chipmunk	4	3	3	1	2		1			1		1
Buccaneer	6		2	4	3	3	4	2	1	2	2	4
Vulcan	2	1	1			1		1		1	1	1
Wessex	3	4	5	4	3	4	4		2	3	4	1
Sycamore	1											
Hastings	1											
Whirlwind	2	5	5	7	3	3	2	2		2	1	
Victor	1		1				1	1		1	1	
Sea Venom		1										
Hunter	2	17	7	6	2	5	3	5	2		6	2
Twin Pioneer		2										
Beverley		2										
Shackleton		3	1									
Britannia		1										
Argosy			1		1							
Harrier				2	3	3	8	5	5	2	4	
Meteor				1								
Belvedere				1								
Phantom				1	1	4	3	5	3	4	1	1
Canberra	5	4	3	2	3	4	2	1				2
Sioux	5	2	3	7	4		2	6	1	9	1	1
Devon		1										

	C1	C2	C3	C4	C5	C6	C7	C8	C9	C10	C11	C12
Wasp	1	3	1	1			1	1		1	1	3
Scout	1	2	1						2		1	
Basset								1				
Varsity	1		1					1				
Sea Heron							1					
Hercules						1						
Sea King			1				1	1	3	1		3
Puma							1	1	1	1	1	
Jaguar									2	2	5	4
Jetstream									1			
Bulldog										1	2	
Pembroke												
Gazelle								1		1	1	3
Andover							1					
Gannet	2	2	2				1	1				
Alouette			1									
Sea Prince						1						
Beaver	1					1			1			
Hiller							1					
Lynx							1					
Auster	1											

	1978	1979	1980	1981	1982	1983	1984	1985	1986	1987	1988	1989	1990
Lightning						1	2	2	1	2	1		
Jet Provost	3	2	2	4	3	2	2	2	2				
Gnat	2	1											
Chipmunk	1		1		1	1							
Beaver	1	1	1			2							
Buccaneer	2	1	1	1	3	1	1	1		1	1		
Vulcan	1												
Wessex	5	3	2	6	9	1	1	1	1	2	1		
Whirlwind			1	1									
Victor					1				1				
Hunter	1	3	3	5	4	1	2				1		2
Argosy							1						
Harrier	1	6	3	3	8	6	2	3	2	4	2	1	
Meteor		1							1		1		
Phantom	4	1	5	1	2	1	1		2	2	4	2	
Canberra	3		1		1	1		1					1
Wasp		1		1	1	4	1	1	1				
Scout	3	3	1		2			2					
Sea King		1	1	4	6	1	3	4	1	2	2	2	
Puma	1	1											
Jaguar	4	6	3	9	5	6	4	4	1	2	1	1	
Jetstream											1	1	
Bulldog	1	1	1	1	1			1	1		1	1	
Pembroke			1										
Gazelle	3	6	4	1	10	3	1		3	3			1
Lynx		1		1	5	1	1	2	4	1	2	2	1
Hawk			2		3	7	5	4	4	2	3	3	1
Harvard					1								
Sea Harrier			1		7	3	2		1	1		2	2

Aircraft									
Chinook			3						2
Nimrod	1			1		1	1	1	
Alouette		1							
Sea Fury				1			1		
Cadet		1							
Tornado		3	3	4	1	3	4	4	4
Vampire			1			1			
Sioux	1								
Tucano									1
Shackleton									1

TOTAL ACCIDENTS (1966-1989)

1966	73	1974	27	1982	76	
1967	64	1975	34	1983	47	
1968	52	1976	39	1984	36	
1969	53	1977	28	1985	28	
1970	43	1978	36	1986	31	
1971	47	1979	43	1987	28	
1972	45	1980	35	1988	24	
1973	45	1981	40	1989	23	

RAF Mid-Air Collisions 1975-90

Date	Aircraft	Mission/Cause	Casualties	Remarks
March 1975	Victor/Buccaneer	Flight refuelling	4K	Victor CAT 5
June 1975	Buccaneer/Buccaneer	High closure rate in turn		1 Buccaneer CAT 5
January 1976	Harrier/Harrier	Post ground-attack manoeuvre	2K	Both CAT 5
April 1976	Gnat/Gnat	Low-level tactical formation	4K	Both CAT 5
September 1979	Harrier/Harrier	Air combat training		Both CAT 5
December 1979	Jaguar/Jaguar	Battle formation	1K	Both CAT 5

Date	Aircraft	Mission/Cause	Casualties	Remarks
May 1980	Jaguar/Jaguar	Formation break to land	1K	Both CAT 5
January 1982	Jaguar/Model a/c	Not known	2K	Model a/c CAT 5
February 1983	Harrier/Harrier	Air combat training		Both CAT 5
June 1983	Jaguar/Jaguar	Formation change		Both CAT 5
July 1983	Hawk/Hawk	Tailchase		Both CAT 5
July 1984	Tornado/Jaguar	Independent low-level sorties		Both CAT 5
February 1985	Harrier/F-104	Independent low-level sorties	1K	Both CAT 5
June 1985	Hercules/Sea King	MRR sortie		Sea King CAT 5
September 1985	Hawk/Hawk	Air combat training		Both CAT 5
October 1985	Jaguar/Jaguar	Low-level battle turn	1K	Both CAT 5
May 1986	Vampire/Meteor	Air display flypast	2K	Both CAT 5
June 1986	Jet Provost/Jet Provost	Air combat training		Both CAT 5
December 1986	Tornado/Tornado	Night formation join-up		1 Tornado CAT 5
June 1987	Tornado/Jaguar	Independent low-level sorties	1K	Both CAT 5
September 1987	Phantom/Phantom	Formation turn		1 Phantom CAT 5
November 1987	Harrier/Harrier	Ground-attack manoeuvre	2K	Both CAT 5
November 1987	Hawk/Hawk	Formation change		Both CAT 5
September 1988	Tornado/Tornado	Independent night sorties	4K	Both CAT 5
January 1989	Tornado/Alpha Jet	Independent training sorties	2K	Both CAT 5
June 1989	Hawk/Hawk	Formation training sortie	1K	Both CAT 5